ANATOMY
of a
DOLL

SUSANNA OROYAN

C&T PUBLISHING

Copyright © 1997 Susanna Oroyan

Developmental Editor: Barbara Konzak Kuhn
Technical Editor: Sally Lanzarotti
Cover Design: John Cram and Kathy Lee
Book Design: Bobbi Sloan Design
Illustrator: Thomas Oroyan
Copy Editor: Judy Moritz

FRONT COVER PHOTOGRAPHS (clockwise from top):
Snow Sprite by Peggy Flynn; 15", cloth. Photo by Mark Carleton.
Ned and Ellie by Kezi Matthews; 14½" and 15½", soft sculpture with wool roving
    hairdo. Photo by Kezi Matthews.
Lady in the Forest by Jane Darin; 21", cotton knit. Photo by Joe Darin.
Joint detail of *Amelia Undressed* by Shelley Thornton; 24", cotton knit, stitched bead
    joints, body joints designed. Photo by Ron Brown.
African Princess by Sandra Feingold; 16", cloth. Photo by Bob Hirsch.
Celestial Seasonings by Julie McCullough; 32", cloth. Photo by John Nollendorfs.
Spirit Seekers by Anne Mayer Meier; 24", fabric. Photo by Photo Pro.
Jester by Akira Blount; 26", linen, cotton. Photo by David Luttrel.

TITLE PAGE PHOTOGRAPH: *Dancing Jesters* by Akiko Anzai; 18", fabric over paperclay.
    Photo by Akiko Anzai.

BACK COVER PHOTOGRAPH: *Mrs. Peepers* by Lisa L. Lichtenfels; detail, nylon over wire
    armature. Photo by Lisa L. Lichtenfels.

Library of Congress Cataloging-in-Publication Data
Oroyan, Susanna

    Anatomy of a doll: a fabric sculptor's handbook / Susanna Oroyan.

    p.   cm.

Includes bibliographical references and index.

ISBN 1-57120-024-X

1. Dollmaking.   2. Cloth dolls.   I. Title.

TT175.07597   1997   96-37077

745.592'21--dc21   CIP

La Doll is a brand name of Padico.
Creative Paperclay is a registered trademark of Creative Paperclay Company, Inc.
Fimo is a registered trademark of Eberhard Faber, Germany.
Lycra is a registered trademark of E.I. duPont de Nemours and Company.
Sculpey and Super Sculpey are registered trademarks of Polyform Products.
Styrofoam Brand Insulation is a registered trademark of Dow Chemical.
Ultrasuede is a registered trademark of Springs Industries, Inc.

Published by C&T Publishing
P.O. Box 1456
Lafayette, California 94549

Printed in China
10 9 8 7 6 5 4 3

DEDICATION
With Thanks

to the 106 artists who generously shared information and photos of their work...

to contributors elinor peace bailey, Barbara Johnston, and Cheiko Ogawa, who helped in the search for artists...

to exhibit coordinators Miriam Gourley, Beverly Dodge Radefeld, and Kathleen Bricker, who made photographic materials available...

to photographers Don Smith, Les Bricker, and Bob Hirsch, who so excellently presented so much of the dollmakers' work...

to special friends of doll art Nancy Lazenby, Katrina Turner, Maralyn Christofferson, and the National Institute of American Doll Artists who graciously loaned photographic materials

and with love and very special thanks

to my husband Tom Oroyan who, once again, has helped make my dreams come true.

The Bride and Her Ghost by Susanna Oroyan; 18", stuffed cotton, cotton over sculpted clay face. Photo by Don Smith.

TABLE
of Contents

DEDICATION 3

PREFACE 6

INTRODUCTION: 8
Designing Original Dolls

SECTION 1:
EVOLUTION OF THE DOLL
What is a Doll? 12
Elemental Forms 14
Primitive Forms 16
Simple Forms 18
Basic Forms 20
The Outline Form 22
The Basic Rag Doll 24
Variations 26

SECTION 2:
THE HEAD
Adding Dimension 28
Turns and Curves 30
Darts and Contours 32
Fully Sculptural 34
Appliquéd Features 36
Beginning Needlesculpture 38
Beginning Stitches 40
Beginning to Sculpt 48
Pressed Cloth 50
Fabric-Covered Sculpture 52
Blended Method
(The Lisa Lichtenfels Head) 54
Masks 58
Painting 60

GALLERY OF FACES 62

Scrap dolls (two versions)
by Virginia Robertson; 8"
to 10", cloth. Photo by
Virginia Robertson.

SECTION 3:
THE BODY

The Basic Body 64

Body Contours 66

Traditional Japanese Body 68

Shaping the Bust 70

Hands 74

Feet 80

The Puzzle Form 82

Patterns by Draping 84

GALLERY OF DOLLS 86

SECTION 4:
BODY JOINTS

Decorative Joints 96

Joint Options 98

The Bead Joint 100

The Stitched Bead Joint 102

The Button Joint 104

SECTION 5:
ASSEMBLIES

Working the Wire 108

The Wire Armature 110

Inserting the Wire 112

Covering the Wire 114

Fixed Figures 116

GALLERY
OF DOLLS 118

SECTION 6:
FINISHING THE
FIGURE

Techniques 128

Hair 130

Shoes 132

Bases 134

Embellishments 136

APPENDIX A

Teaching Yourself the ABC's of
Dollmaking 138

APPENDIX B

Sources 141

Artists 141

Supplies 142

Bibliography 142

About the Author 143

Index 144

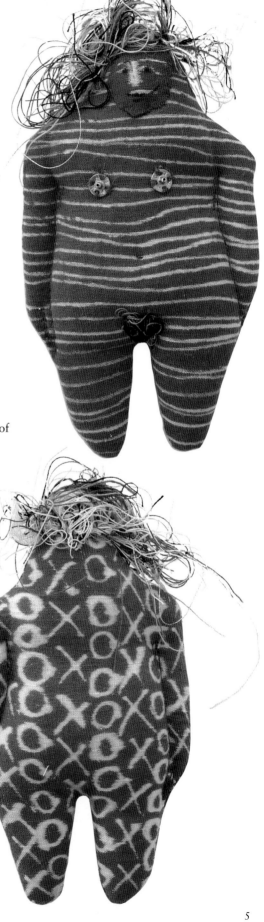

Sewing Basket Doll (front and back) by Margi Hennen; 8" to 10", cloth. Photo by Warren Dodgson.

Of Winter Fields Lately (two versions) by Margi Hennen; 8" to 10". Photo by Warren Dodgson.

As a teacher and writer in the field of dollmaking, I am often asked questions such as, "I have a head and hands, where can I find out how to put them together?" or "I want to make a doll with a bust, where can I learn how this is done?" In most cases the questioners do not want to be referred to a specific pattern or project book because they do not want to take the time to work through another's design. They just want to know the particular technique or set of techniques that they can incorporate into their own projects. The problem for me in answering them is that there are usually several possible approaches. I find myself saying, "You could do this, or this, or if you did that, you could do this," which is a little too much for the questioner to take in all at once. Often the conversation ends with both of us saying, "I wish we had a standard reference book that could cover all the bases."

This book is an attempt to outline as many methods of doll construction as possible, so that beginning or working dollmakers have a handy answer book. The book might best be described as a technical reference book with expansion capabilities: a workbook to help dollmakers develop ideas. When you think, I want to make a pressed felt head, how can I do this?, you should be able to find a few basic approaches within the sections. Then, I hope, you will invent, create, expand, or change the idea using your imagination.

Dollmaking is a multi-media construction. It really doesn't make any difference which type of dollmaker you are, or want to be. Nor does it make any difference which particular technique you choose. The main considerations when making a doll are to understand the desired effect or impression you want to make, then to be willing to play with variations of your idea and explore any directions that are suggested. And to take into consideration the effects of a technique when you use or manipulate a certain material. This book explains how to achieve certain effects and helps to answer the "what happens if..." questions.

I hope you will find the material useful for practice, for play, or for reference when solving a problem. Use the book as a practice manual or exercise book. If you're a beginner, work through the exercises that relate to the outlined techniques in order to teach yourself a good, general course in dollmaking. If you have some experience with dollmaking, try the techniques that are unfamiliar to you—at the very least, the result would be learning those which you did not like, or those that you found uncomfortable. At best, you will have given yourself an enlarged repertoire of possibilities to draw from when solving design problems.

As you work through the sections, you'll find that many, many artists shared photographs of their work in order to expose a reader to the equivalent of four or five gallery exhibits. In most cases the photographs accompanying the sections show examples of that method, but, do note, they are often variations on the theme. Artists being artists, they "do their own thing." Accordingly, use the photo examples as a guide for your own inventions by studying where the stitches are placed and how the parts are shaped. Also study the number of possible variations that can happen using just one method, and think about how many techniques you can identify on just one piece. Looking, studying, and experimenting are the ways that most of us learned to do what we do...and so can you.

Unless otherwise noted, the drawings and diagrams are either generic forms (not an integral part of a copyrighted or patented pattern), or they are parts of original patterns or models that I have developed. In most cases the pattern shapes will not be directly usable to create specific finished doll forms. Either reproduce or copy the shapes to use as an aid or as a basis for variation when developing your own designs.

Always remember that there is no clock running and no graded test at the end. None of us got it right the first, second, or even the forty-second time. The goal is to have fun and to feel the rewards of figuring out how to make your idea real. Experiment and enjoy!

Homage to Erica Jong by Lois Schklar; 18", cloth. Photo by Les Bricker.

FACING PAGE: *Alya, the Child's Creative Spirit* by Gretchen Lima; 21", fabric, hard sculpted hands. Photo by Bill Lemke.

Designing Original Dolls

THE CREATIVE PROCESS

This book is full of pictures, pattern shapes, and drawings of technical details: lots of parts and images that you can use to create forms with your hands. You'll see how to bend wire this way, cut cloth that way, sew them together this or that way. What is this all for? Designing your original dolls.

In order to access the materials presented, you need to use your mind. You will need to have an idea, or a feeling for the specific expression of that idea, and some understanding of the basic principles of design. You will have to have a general idea of what you want to happen so you can put together methods and materials to achieve the best expression.

Some of you have made original dolls already. You probably took a look and said, "I've never done a jointed doll or inserted an armature, so I think I'll try that." Some may never have tried to make a doll without a pattern, but are just itching to try. And some of you are saying, "Hey, wait a minute, I can't create an original design, I'm not creative." Yet creativity and design are abilities everyone has. If you are one who doubts her own potential, say to yourself, "I am and I can," and read on.

First, you need to think about who you are, and you need to have an idea. Neither of these are scary. To begin, you might say, "I am a person who makes, or wants to make, small representations of human beings that people might call dolls." The so-called creative person will just go make them whether he or she knows anything about creating a form or not. For these people, the wanting to do it is stronger than anything else. They will figure it out, trying and failing, until they get what they want. To the uninitiated this looks like work. To the people who do it, it is actually useful fun. They enjoy trying out new ideas and learning from their mistakes.

However, self-styled noncreative individuals will hesitate because they think there must be a right way, or because they are afraid to fail, or because they think all the good ideas have been used already. Let's get rid of this old baggage. There is no such thing as a right way. Whatever works for you is the right way. If whatever you feel works is right, then no one but you can say whether you failed. Self-criticism is good, but only if constructive. Say to yourself, "This isn't as good as I wanted, so I will do it over again differently, and this time I will do X instead of Y." Always remember you are in control. Artwork is self-satisfaction. The best artists are the ones who are always looking to improve something or to do it differently.

Ideas are pretty much universal. We all identify with the idea of historical figures, characters, pretty ladies, social and cultural events, and the general shapes—real or abstract—of the human body. It is your variation and interpretation of these ideas that make your work original or creative. The very minute you notice (see, hear, feel, read about) something in your environment, you have an idea that can become a doll. Two people drinking coffee in a restaurant or one piece of interesting fabric can be an idea for a doll. Opinions, emotional reactions, and personal preferences can be ideas, too.

For a recent challenge exhibit, dollmakers were given the theme of Shakespeare's play *A Midsummer Night's Dream* and a selection of four fabric patterns to use. The results varied from traditional figures in Renaissance costume, to fairies and elves, to a wall, a bonfire spirit, and even tree figures. Each artist personally reacted to some particular element of the play or made a unique connection between the play and the color and pattern of the fabrics.

For a dollmaker, creativity is essentially the ability to manipulate the elements of an idea. The "tools" for the manipulation are questions you ask yourself throughout the process. Sounds fairly heavy duty, but creativity can be learned!

THE DESIGN PROCESS

Let's take a look at doll design. When making dolls, we are concerned with these major elements of design: form, color, texture, pattern, scale, proportion, mechanics, and expression. Form is the shape of the figure you want to make in dollmaking, which also includes that very important element of mechanics, or answering the question, "I want this shape, how will I put the pieces together to get the shape?"

Scene from *A Midsummer Night's Dream* by Christine Shively; 16", cloth, wood, needlesculpture. Photo by Azad.

Scene from *A Midsummer Night's Dream: Mustard Seed, Stray Sod, and Stout as the Wall* by Brenda Gehl; 6" to 16", cloth, various media. Brenda Gehl accepted the challenge and used the products to create a very different and very unique interpretation of three of the characters in Shakespeare's play. Photo by Azad.

human figure. For example, if you were to do a figure for a doll house that was built on a one-inch-equals-one-foot scale, it would become very important to size all body parts and clothing to that scale.

Proportion enters in when you begin to distort or abstract. Proportion means that there is a balance given to the design elements. For example, one large element would be balanced by two small elements. A good example is seen in my Ample Annie design (*Ladies in the Steam Bath,* see page 72). Annie's major emphasis is her big, bulky torso. In order to maintain and emphasize the image, I purposely made her head, hands, and feet in a smaller scale. Another purposeful choice in Annie is the lack of detail in her hands and feet. If her hands and feet had fingers and toes, the viewer's eye would tend to spend a little more time examining the detail. Similarly, if her face had been painted or needlesculpted in detail, the viewer would get carried away with a character interpretation. The message Annie wants to project is "large," and all elements are scaled, balanced, and proportioned to underline that message. Additional messages in Annie are determined by the clothing (or lack of it).

Mechanics and expression are the elements that connect creativity and design. You use them when you decide which method of construction will give maximum expression to your idea.

Color is the choice of a set of colors that appear to coordinate with each other or to enhance a dominant color. It is also the choice of colors to portray a message. It can be the choice of colors used in unexpected ways to jar the viewer. In western culture, for example, a bride dressed in black would certainly be contrary to expectations. Put a baby in a white dress with lots of ribbons and laces, and you would be underlining and emphasizing the idea of "cute baby."

Texture is usually thought of as the dimensional surface of a material, but it can also be things applied to a surface. We choose specific types of fabric to deliver particular messages that underline the idea of the doll. Polished cotton creates a slick and hard look, velvet a soft look, and slubbed linen a rather rough, homespun look. Metal and leather can convey hard, dangerous, or crude appearances, or a bright, slick, and chic appearance, depending on the type used. Adding paint or embroidery for dimension can also add texture.

Pattern is repetition or variation of similar elements. Beads may form a pattern. Buttons may form a pattern. Changes in colors or the color of repetitive shapes can create pattern.

Scale refers to making a figure conform in all parts to a specific size. Scale usually enters into dollmaking when there is a specific desire to create a realistic

St. John's Eve Bonfire by Susanna Oroyan; 14", cloth over wire. Photo by Susanna Oroyan. The Bonfire figure was created to show the products of four different manufacturers, using the challenge theme. Traditionally, bonfires were built on Midsummer Night, so orange fabric was chosen as the ground. Gold paints, glitters, and metallic ribbons were used to emphasize the idea of flame. The end result is that the figure personifies fire.

Angel by Susanna Oroyan; 18", wire, beads. Photo by Don Smith.

All the elements of design mentioned are based on the pleasing and efficient organization we observe in nature: the placement of leaves on a twig, the whorls of a shell, the patterns of crystals, an animal's coloration, the way limbs are arranged on a human being to allow movement. We tend to imitate these satisfactory organizations or the design of nature when we make things. But in order to do this, we have to invent construction methods that fit our desired expression. For instance, our bodies' limbs are moved with joints, muscles, and tendons. In a doll we have to use other materials, such as wire, thread, and buttons, to imitate joint action.

FINDING YOUR IDEA

Let's go back to the concept of ideas and the questions we must ask ourselves in the process of design. Once upon a time I was sculpting with no particular character in mind. After awhile, I got the idea that the head shape had sort of an angelic expression. I thought maybe he/she wanted to be an angel. Then I asked myself, "What is an angel?" Scholars have worked on that question for centuries, but the answer that popped up for me was: a creature of light. My next question: how do I make a doll of hard and soft materials look like light? The key words here are to "make" or "put together," which equals mechanics, materials, and expression. Light, however, indicates absence of material, so the problem now became how to make something without materials. The answer was to make it with as few raw materials as possible and use them to suggest emptiness. The final figure was composed of a sculpted head, hands, and a chest connected with wires, so light passes through it. The figure was made to be suspended—lightweight—and was embellished with many fine wires and bright, sparkly beads—reflected light. (If you see an angel as a winged creature, then your design suggestions will probably have to do with how to make and attach wings.) My definition of the idea suggested the required mechanics.

With the figure called *Motherhood*, the initial idea was one of a mother weighted down by her children's needs (a heavy, plodding figure). At first I saw this as a hard, sculpted figure on a fixed wire armature body. Then I saw the idea as a woman who is carrying on with her responsibilities, as messy and demanding as they may be. Since I didn't have to work with the idea of weight, I could choose to make the figure in cloth. I chose not to use color so that the positions of the figures would convey the expression. If I am successful, the viewer knows without being told the name that the idea of motherhood is being expressed. The viewer can project his or her positive or negative reaction onto the figures. You could do this same idea and needlesculpt or paint a radiant face or a dejected one. Pick what the idea requires. As you use this book, you will be working with your idea to find the best method of expressing your idea mechanically.

Ideas can be doodles, phrases, or mental images. Ideas can be fragments. For instance, you might see a picture of a big red hat and think, I like that idea, what kind of a doll would look good in that big red hat? Picking the type will depend on your tastes. You might be more inclined to see a pretty lady in a big red hat than a wizened elf.

So, you can see that creativity involves some serious thinking about the elements of design in order to enhance an idea and its particular message.

Can you learn to do this? Sure you can. Following someone else's pattern is a wonderful learning tool. It teaches you particular methods, and if you analyze what you are being told to do, it should teach you to understand the designer's thought processes and/or to be critical of them. The way you start is to concentrate on independent thinking. When you follow a pattern, but still choose your own favorite fabric patterns and finishing details, such as hairstyles and wig materials, you are being independent. You are designing. Those choices are based on what you like or want. Finding an idea or vision you like, even if a little part is applied to another's pattern, is the start of being creative.

Many people believe that to be creative you must sit down and sketch up a complete idea right out of thin air. Mistaken notion. Who says patterns are required to spring out fully detailed? Many dollmakers just cut the fabric freehand, sew it, and see if it works; if it doesn't, they change, cut, and sew it until it does.

Creative design usually starts with "What if?" What if...I use this shape of hand? If I do use this shape of hand, what sort of head do I use? Or, it might start with a piece of fabric. What kind of doll or costume does it suggest? When you answer questions for yourself, you are using your imagination creatively. When you ask and answer a number of questions, applying some consideration to the elements of design, you are being creative.

I should note that being creative or considering the elements of dollmaking does not make art, or an idea good, or the design successful. The end product is based on the quality of work or the personal vision and how much the maker wants to work to refine his or her personal vision into a very tightly integrated, well-designed and well-defined artistic statement. Being creative means giving yourself the freedom to explore, the freedom to fail, and the permission to try again.

DECIDING CHARACTER

Millions of words can be written, have been written, in an attempt to define art and the elements which make the piece. For dolls, it seems to me that two words suffice: depth and power; in particular, depth and power as they relate to the expression of human character or personality in the piece. The play doll probably needs to move, probably has removable clothes, but most importantly, it allows the player to decide who the character is. The art doll is expected to tell the viewer, hint strongly, or make the viewer think about certain aspects of the human condition. Both pieces need to please, educate, or amuse the viewer. At the very least, they need to provoke an emotion or intellectual reaction that will hold the viewer's attention for longer than a passing moment. The more thought that

goes into the design and construction of a piece (depth), the more likely there will be an evocative or provocative reaction (power).

As you get to the finished product, "What if..." is still the main question. Use a number of directional phrases to point yourself toward solutions. Creativity is problem solving. A great deal of it should happen before you even start to work. I make 90% of my dolls while kicking back in a comfortable chair, feet up on the desk, with my eyes closed. I like working the problem out as much as possible by running a mental movie of the idea and solving the "What happens if..." questions with as little expense of time, material, and energy as possible. I might run my mental movie a week—or three—taking time out to check my fabric boxes or look up costume references. Sometimes, but not often, I will actually make a sketch or notes.

Here is a list of just a few directional words you can use to help with solutions for making your ideas real and designs workable: stretch, expand, narrow, reduce, lighten, darken, shade, contrast, reverse, mix, break, bend, contract, multiply. As you work on your design, you will find you can identify many other change words.

What happens if you...

stretch the leg,

expand the waist,

insert wire,

joint the limbs,

lighten the fabric (choose a lighter color, a lighter weight),

reverse the print (use the wrong side),

needlesculpt the face,

paint the face,

multiply the number of buttons,

mix the colors together,

expand the size of the limbs,

well, what happens is...

you create a new doll form!

Motherhood by Susanna Oroyan; 20", cloth. Photo by Les Bricker.

What is a Doll?

Do you really know what a doll is? I am sure I don't. The best description we can offer is that a doll seems to be a representation of the human figure. People make dolls and like dolls because they are interested in other people, what they do, how they look, what they wear, how they feel...a doll is just another way we appreciate the infinite variety of our fellow humans. When you consider the creation of dolls, there is really nothing new under the sun in dollmaking. Most of the techniques used in dollmaking can be traced back at least 100 years, and in many cases, 200 to 300 years. What makes doll-making an ever changing, always fascinating art form is that the subject matter, humans, can be seen and thought of in a never-ending multitude of ways. Also, the artists who portray dolls continue to be inventive and exciting by varying the techniques with differing shapes, materials, and surface treatment combinations.

The question of why humans want to make representations of themselves leads us to some interesting theories. Could it have been because the early woman gave her girl child a baby-like toy to train her for future maternal duties? Could it have been because a man

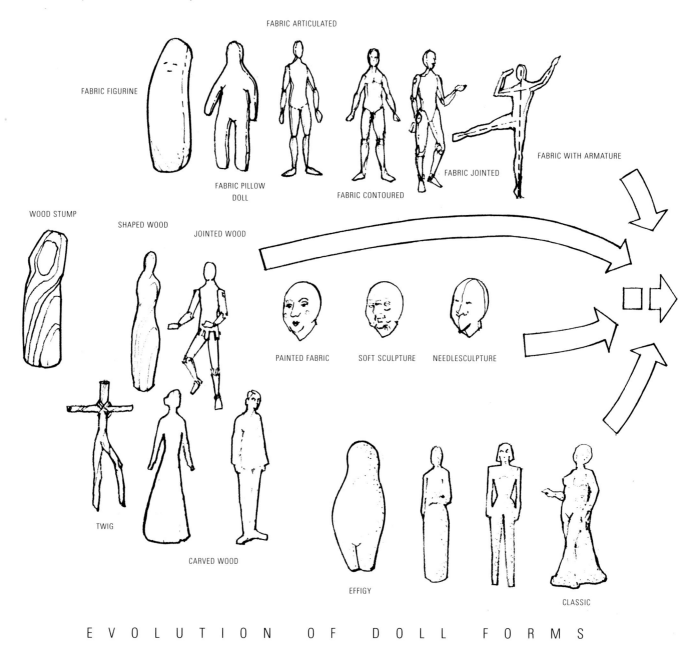

FABRIC ARTICULATED

FABRIC FIGURINE

FABRIC PILLOW DOLL

FABRIC CONTOURED

FABRIC JOINTED

FABRIC WITH ARMATURE

WOOD STUMP

SHAPED WOOD

JOINTED WOOD

PAINTED FABRIC

SOFT SCULPTURE

NEEDLESCULPTURE

TWIG

CARVED WOOD

EFFIGY

CLASSIC

E V O L U T I O N   O F   D O L L   F O R M S

wanted a figure to represent a great hunter who might bring him luck and bravery? Although we will never know for sure, we can see how the child-occupier became today's toy and the talisman became a religious figure. Whenever the maker had no apparent reason for making a figure, but did so anyhow for the sheer joy of creating, we have the purely esthetic or art doll figure.

How we make these "little people" seems to have evolved in two different ways. On one hand, a form can begin from a solid, sculpted figure, or an elemental form, which we might call a statue or figurine. On the other hand, a form can begin by joining two pieces of fabric together and adding padding to make a dimensional form, or an outline form, which we might call a cookie cutter or pillow doll. From this form, a flat form evolves when the two pieces of cloth are manipulated by turning the flat parts, by seaming the curves, by needlesculpting, by jointing, by molding the cloth over a solid base, or by inserting armatures or other materials, in order to create a three-dimensional surface.

From the solid, sculpted figure, the doll form devolves when the sculpture is broken up or manipulated so that the form can show movement. The figure is cut apart to make joints, or it is cut into major sculpted parts which are then assembled on a body made of another material. You can think of these processes as breaking down from one side and building up from the other.

It seems that dollmaking is often thought of in terms of "either/or." It either involves some form of solid sculpted work, or, it requires some form of fabric assembly. The truth is that most dollmaking falls within a large middle area where elements of both meet. A good dollmaker will use any element that will work for the design. For example, cured or fired sculpture pieces might be assembled on a body constructed of cloth, stuffing, and wire.

You should become at least familiar with, if not experienced with, as many techniques as possible in order to solve design problems that might occur while you're working between the first idea and the finished piece.

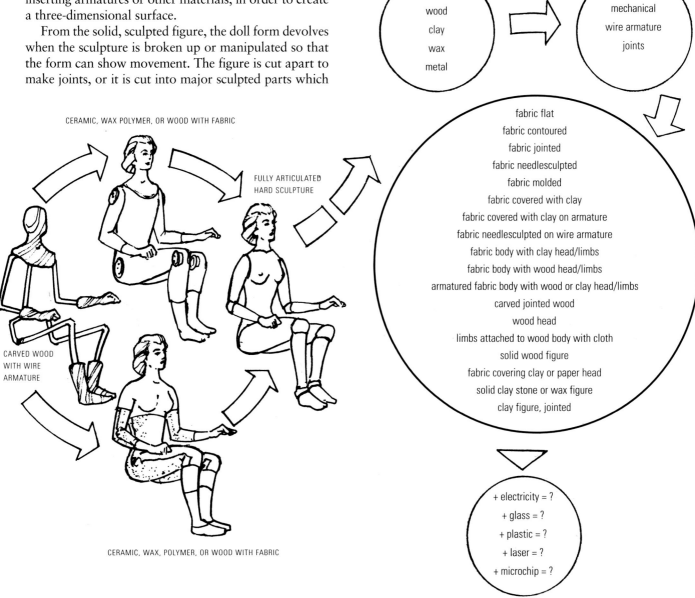

CERAMIC, WAX POLYMER, OR WOOD WITH FABRIC

FULLY ARTICULATED HARD SCULPTURE

CARVED WOOD WITH WIRE ARMATURE

CERAMIC, WAX, POLYMER, OR WOOD WITH FABRIC

fabrics
wood
clay
wax
metal

mechanical
wire armature
joints

fabric flat
fabric contoured
fabric jointed
fabric needlesculpted
fabric molded
fabric covered with clay
fabric covered with clay on armature
fabric needlesculpted on wire armature
fabric body with clay head/limbs
fabric body with wood head/limbs
armatured fabric body with wood or clay head/limbs
carved jointed wood
wood head
limbs attached to wood body with cloth
solid wood figure
fabric covering clay or paper head
solid clay stone or wax figure
clay figure, jointed

+ electricity = ?
+ glass = ?
+ plastic = ?
+ laser = ?
+ microchip = ?

Elemental Forms

Almost every society and culture has a history of using elemental materials—commonly stone, wood, clay, wax, hide, or bone, depending on the location—to make dolls. Nowadays, we lump these natural elements with everyday items and call them all "found" materials. Today's dollmakers still play with these elemental forms; we see this in mascots, little fetishes, wearable figures, and even larger abstract figures. None of these forms require instructions or patterns because they are usually created by assembling an assortment of materials, moving them around, noting the suggested form, and combining the materials to accentuate the form.

It is interesting to theorize which came first—the form or the idea for the form. Did the shape of the twig suggest the figure of a person, or did the maker decide on a person figure, pick up a handy twig, and make it? Assuming the human thought process doesn't change much, it was probably a little of each—a little wanting to make something and a little of seeing something suggested in a natural material.

For the individual, or for the group, a dollmaking challenge based on found materials can be exciting, therapeutic, and surely a non-threatening way of enjoying how to make dolls.

Pulling Up Roots by Tracy Page Stillwell; 18", dyed fabrics, clay, found materials. Photo by Beth Ludwig.

Clarity by Tracy Page Stillwell; 26", fabric, clay, found materials. Photo by Beth Ludwig.

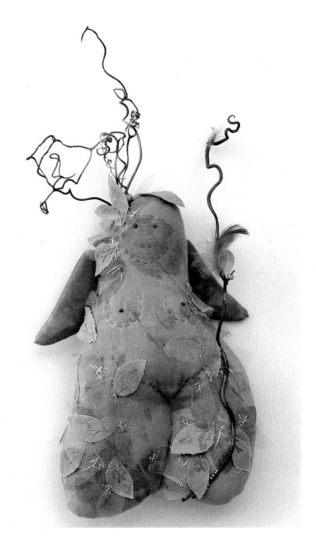

Not a Chance: Spirit of the Fine Frosty Friday by Margi Hennen; 10", leaf printed cloth, embroidery, found materials. Photo by Warren Dodgson.

The results of combining found items to create elemental forms make inexpensive but unique gifts, decor, and ornaments. When made of local natural materials, the dolls can even be sold as tourist souvenirs.

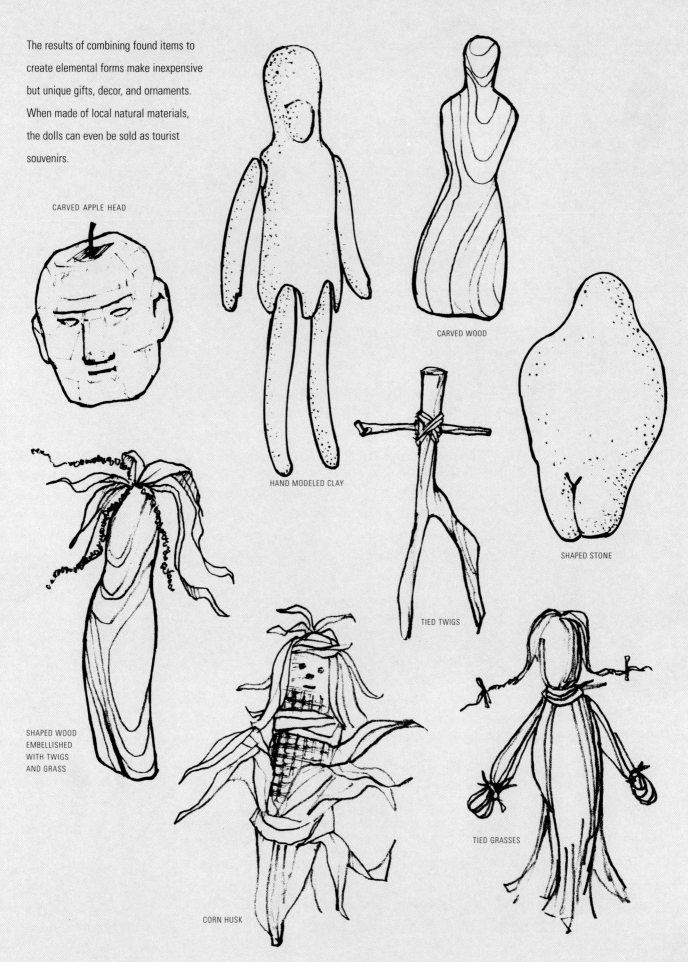

CARVED APPLE HEAD

CARVED WOOD

HAND MODELED CLAY

SHAPED STONE

TIED TWIGS

SHAPED WOOD EMBELLISHED WITH TWIGS AND GRASS

CORN HUSK

TIED GRASSES

Primitive Forms

Dolls defy a neat evolutionary scale of classification. However, if we say that the "first" cloth figure was made by wrapping, tying, or draping a woven material to make a variation on an assembled elemental figure, then primitive dolls are best described as the adaptation of the elemental found-material forms to the manufactured products of civilization.

Wrapped yarn doll with woven dress by Barbara Evans; 8", yarn. Photo by Barbara Evans.

Wrapped yarn dolls by Barbara Evans; 6", yarn. Photo by Barbara Evans.

Handkerchief doll by Barbara Evans; 6", cloth. Photo by Barbara Evans.

Felt doll by Barbara Evans; 8", felt. Photo by Barbara Evans.

All of the forms are made by folding, wrapping, and tying. Although no stitches are necessary, do note that sewing is basically a method of wrapping and knotting. We just work today in more elaborate patterns with tools, much finer threads, and sophisticated machinery.

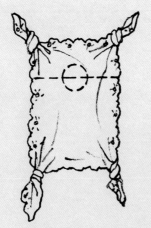

The handkerchief doll shows how a doll form can be created from a flat piece of woven material. Place a pad of stuffing to form the head, tie a string around the "neck", then tie the corners to make hands and feet.

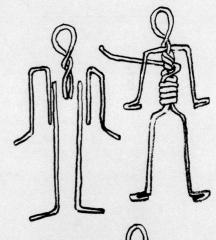

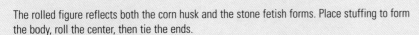

The rolled figure reflects both the corn husk and the stone fetish forms. Place stuffing to form the body, roll the center, then tie the ends.

The wire figure is a variation of the skeletal form of a twig doll. Bend wire or pipe cleaners to the desired shape, then wrap the torso to create thickness in form.

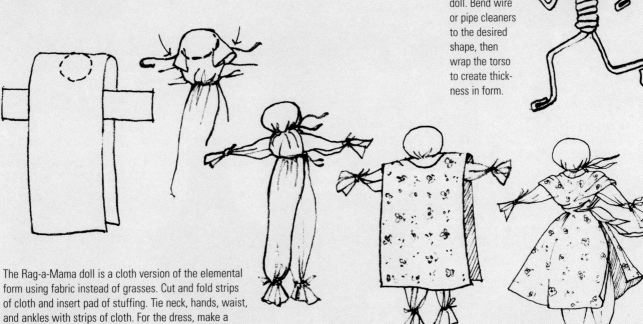

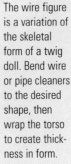

The Rag-a-Mama doll is a cloth version of the elemental form using fabric instead of grasses. Cut and fold strips of cloth and insert pad of stuffing. Tie neck, hands, waist, and ankles with strips of cloth. For the dress, make a hole in a piece of cloth and tie around the waist.

Simple Forms

PMS Doll (right) pin by Elaine Anne Spence and doll pin (left) in author's collection; 3" to 4", cloth. Photo by Susanna Oroyan.

Almost every dollmaker has played with the simple form and variations on that theme. Simple forms may be seen to fall between the non-sculpted, stitchless primitive form and the more sophisticated, engineered figure. Since the forms require a minimum of sewing and technical skill, a dollmaker can quickly create and construct a form that can then be embellished or given greater character. Personality is applied by embellishing with paints, patches, beads, or whatever strikes the maker's fancy.

Ofuku-san by Sizuyo Ogawa; 8", Ogawa's large pieces are built over bottles. Wonderfully textured and patterned Japanese fabrics are wrapped and stitched over the bottle form to portray traditional costumes. Photo by Masayuki Tsutsui.

Friendship pin by Althea Church; 3", cloth. Photo by Althea Church.

Leprechaun and *Two Little Girls with Their Dollies* by Jane Wagner; approx. 1", cloth. Jane Wagner makes her tiny two-piece dolls by machine sewing the basic form with felt. Photo by Richard Wagner, Jr.

Flutterbyes pin by Louise Mendenhall; 5", cloth. Photo by Louise Mendenhall.

Three artist-designed pins in the author's collection; 3" to 5", cloth. Photo by Susanna Oroyan.

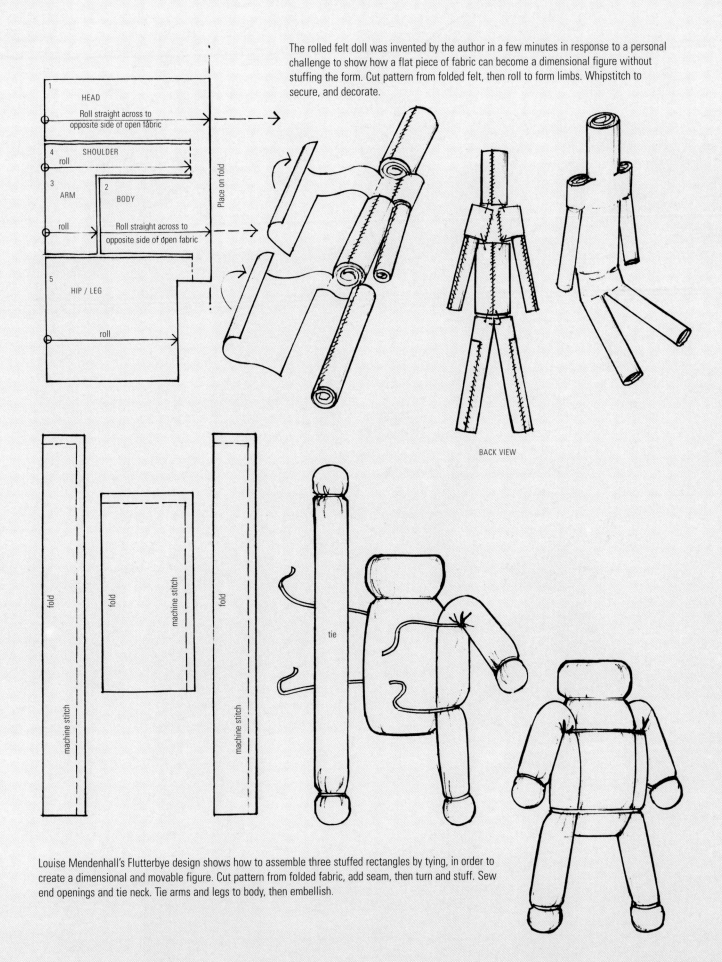

The rolled felt doll was invented by the author in a few minutes in response to a personal challenge to show how a flat piece of fabric can become a dimensional figure without stuffing the form. Cut pattern from folded felt, then roll to form limbs. Whipstitch to secure, and decorate.

1 HEAD
Roll straight across to opposite side of open fabric

4 SHOULDER
roll

3 ARM
roll

2 BODY
Roll straight across to opposite side of open fabric

5 HIP / LEG
roll

Place on fold

BACK VIEW

fold

machine stitch

fold

machine stitch

fold

machine stitch

tie

Louise Mendenhall's Flutterbye design shows how to assemble three stuffed rectangles by tying, in order to create a dimensional and movable figure. Cut pattern from folded fabric, add seam, then turn and stuff. Sew end openings and tie neck. Tie arms and legs to body, then embellish.

Basic Forms

At this stage of doll-making a bit of design enters in. Instead of assembling found materials, or manipulating given forms, we are now beginning to think about creating shape ourselves and controlling the outcome of the product. For most of us, creating a simple form happens about the time we try to stitch two pieces of shaped fabric together. It certainly happens when we also stuff some other material between the two pieces to add dimension. The key word is now "shape." Although the pieces might just be squares, triangles, rectangles, or stars, will we make them long or short, will they become flat or round, or will they become a combination of several shapes?

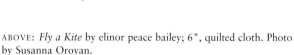

ABOVE: *Fly a Kite* by elinor peace bailey; 6", quilted cloth. Photo by Susanna Oroyan.

UPPER RIGHT: *Star Ladies* by Sally Lampi; 7", star shapes of painted cloth. Sally created a very strong illusion of motion by curving and elongating the points of the star. Photo by Sally Lampi.

LOWER RIGHT: *African Princess* by Sandra Feingold; 16", cloth. A rectangular form is well-used to set off the strong diagonal stripes of Sandra's *African Princess* doll. Photo by Bob Hirsch.

The sketches shown on this page give us a small sample of what a designer can do with just a pencil, straight edge, and compass.

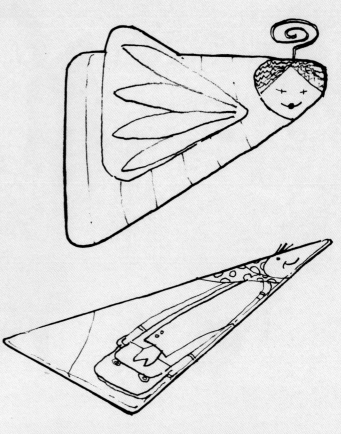

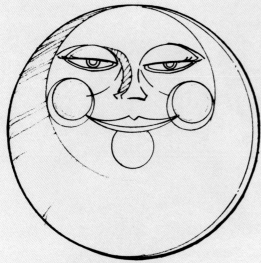

elinor peace bailey developed the famous Flying Phoebe form by playing with the triangle idea of the folded paper airplane.

These sketched star figures show how two very different forms develop from a basic five-pointed star form.

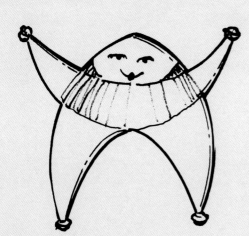

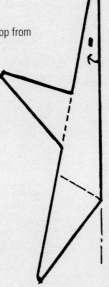

The Outline Form

Another simple doll shape is the outline form, which can be called the pillow doll or cookie cutter doll. The outline form takes shape when we cut two pieces of fabric to outline a specifically human shape, sew them together with right sides (printed or finished sides) of the fabric facing, turn the piece inside out so the raw seam edges are on the inside, and stuff to give the form dimension. Although these steps seem simple, they actually involve some complex problem solving when we have to decide how to create the shape, hide the raw edges, insert the stuffing, and select the material to use for stuffing. When selecting the fabrics and finishes, the maker also needs to have specialized tools, such as scissors, pencils, needles, and a sewing machine to construct the form. Maybe there is no such thing as a simple basic form!

Many artists have created very powerful art pieces working with the outline form. Sometimes the effect comes from surface embellishment, but usually it comes from expanding or varying the outline of the piece. Depending on the maker's ability to draw an interesting shape and to manipulate the fabric for curves that the shape might require, a high degree of motion, and emotion, can be communicated with the outline form.

Angel by Sally Lampi; 10", needlesculpted cloth. Photo by Sally Lampi.

Matron Saint of Safe Credit by Margi Hennen; 13", beading on cotton. Photo by Warren Dodgson.

Spirit Seekers by Anne Mayer Meier; 24", fabric with modeled clay faces. Photo by Photo Pro.

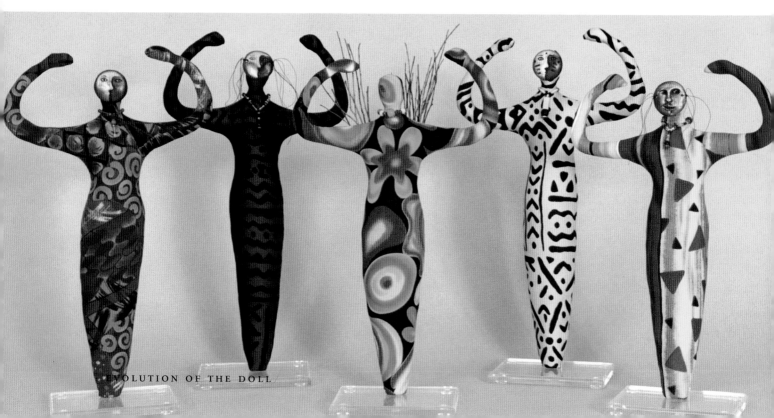

Pillow shapes, or shapes with simple, large outlines, can be used for decorations or displayed as mounted sculptural pieces. More simply outlined forms are often created as play dolls for children, and smaller forms easily become wearables.

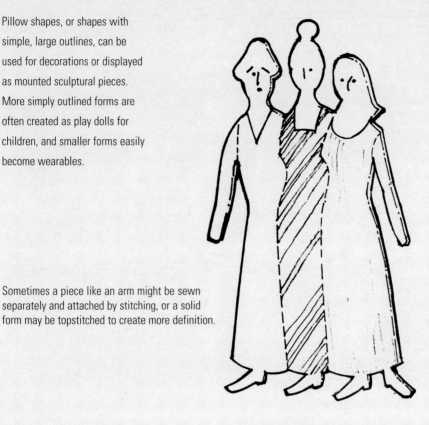

Sometimes a piece like an arm might be sewn separately and attached by stitching, or a solid form may be topstitched to create more definition.

Patterns for outline forms are created by first making a drawing of the desired doll. Add the seam allowances to the drawing.

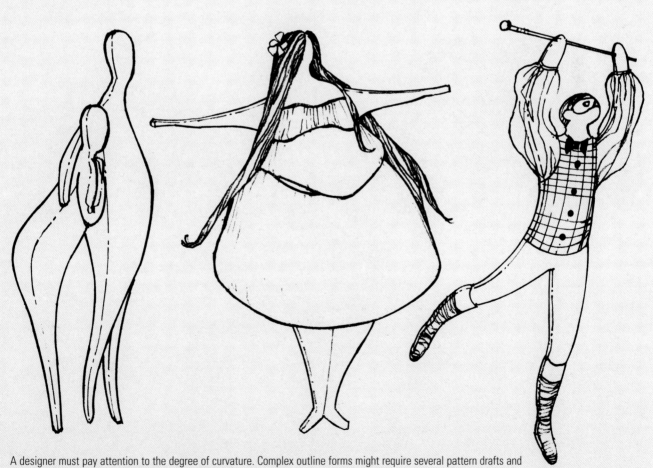

A designer must pay attention to the degree of curvature. Complex outline forms might require several pattern drafts and model revisions to make a successful form. Note that two outline shapes may be combined.

The Basic Rag Doll

The basic rag doll, a traditional flat form, can be considered the great-grandmother of cloth dolls. This doll is purposely built for "flop and fun." During play, a child often imposes the character and action on the doll—the form doesn't have to do anything in particular. After awhile though, the doll usually starts bending in the narrow areas, such as the neck, hips, and ankles. Working with this tendency to bend, many dollmakers find themselves taking the first steps toward making a jointed three-dimensional form when they compose this form.

Dressing Up by Rebecca Swanson; 14", cloth. Photo by Don Smith.

Basic Doll II by Betty Ballentine; 22", cloth. Photo by Betty Ballentine.

Nosalie and Noodles by Carol-Lynn Rössel Waugh; 15", cloth. Photo by Carol-Lynn Rössel Waugh.

Bridget by Virginia Black; 10", cloth. Photo by Virginia Black.

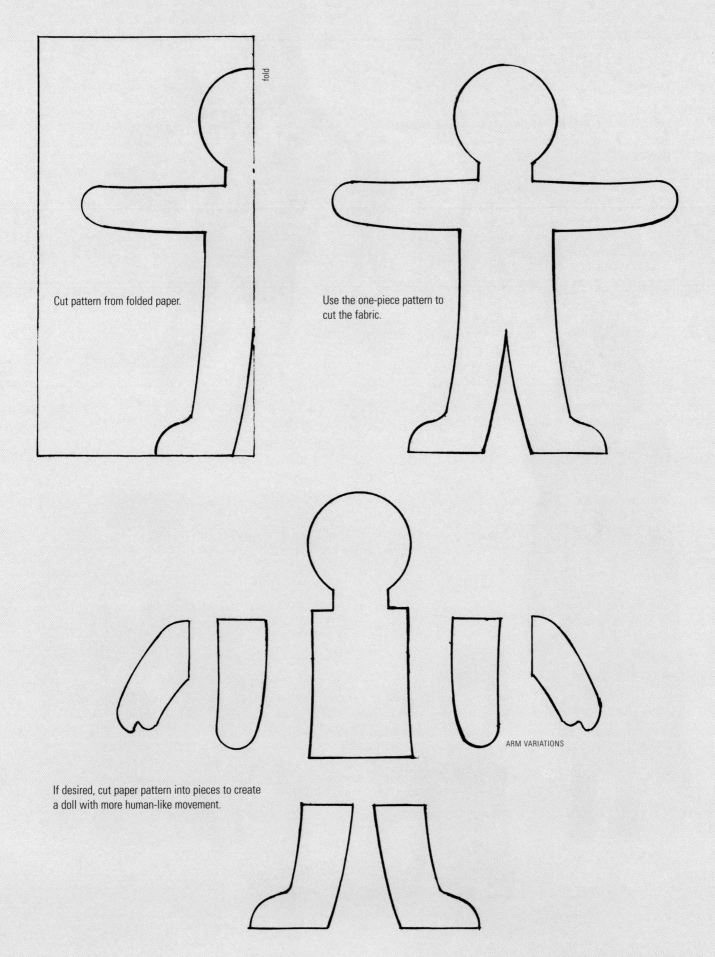

fold

Cut pattern from folded paper.

Use the one-piece pattern to cut the fabric.

ARM VARIATIONS

If desired, cut paper pattern into pieces to create a doll with more human-like movement.

Variations

Here is where real fun begins! As you view the photographs, you will notice that there are many ways to make very complex figures in cloth. The marvel of dollmaking is that inventive and imaginative dollmakers put materials together in their own unique ways, and you quite often have to look very closely to see the basic form. The reality is that 80% to 90% of all cloth dolls are variations of the basic rag doll form.

From this point forward, there is no particular order of the possible variations for dollmaking. You are like a squirrel standing in the fork of a tree. You can select any branch, run out to the end of any twig, then leap across to a different branch. It is your choice as a designer of dolls.

Bliss the Twisted Sister by Elaine Anne Spence; 15", cloth. Consider the way Elaine uses the rag doll form as an abstract expression. Photo by Bill Bachhuber.

Eva by Norma Malerich; 33", cloth. Consider how Norma uses the rag doll form as a ground for making a painting. Photo by Norma Malerich.

Sophie by Susanna Oroyan; 48", cloth. Sophie is just the basic rag form enlarged to 48" tall and given a more curved foot. Photo by Don Smith.

The Donkey and the Elephant by Sandy Belt; 15", cloth. Note how Sandy adjusts the rag doll form to create animal whimsies. Photo by Christine Garcew.

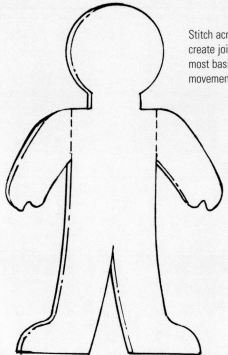

Stitch across the stuffed form to create joint bends. This creates the most basic joint and allows for movement in the doll.

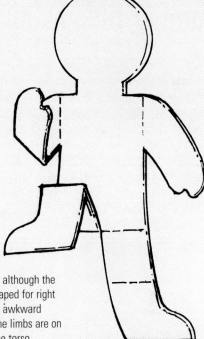

The doll can now sit, although the hands and feet, if shaped for right and left, will point in awkward directions because the limbs are on the same plane as the torso.

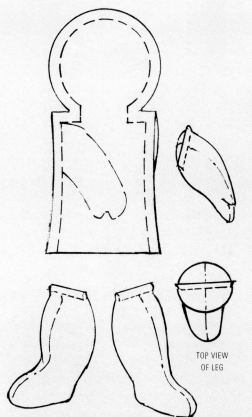

TOP VIEW
OF LEG

The stitched joint allows the limb to move in a fully circular, non-human motion, which may allow too much flop. This type of a joint gives a lot of scope for play poses, but, when hand stitched, may require the maker to repair attachments from time to time if the doll is used by an active child.

Usually the solution is to turn the legs so that the feet point out in front of the body and the arms are turned so that they hang naturally at the sides of the body. When the machine-sewn figure is turned right side out, the toes and fingers will point in the right direction. Length of the limbs can be adjusted for the design.

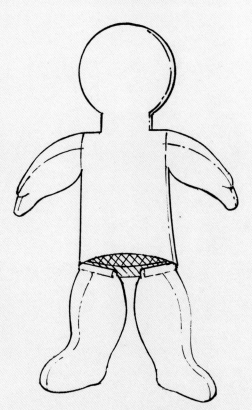

Cut apart the pattern and re-attach the limbs in order to create more acceptable human-like positions for the hands and feet. Add extra seam allowance at the top of the leg and arm pieces, then sew each limb together. Turn under the raw edges, sew the ends, and stitch to the body.

An alternative solution is to position the limbs at a quarter turn (90°) to the body, then sew the separate parts into the seam between the two body pieces.

Adding Dimension

To make dolls look more human, most dollmakers like to add depth or dimension to their pieces. For the head, the first step toward adding dimension is simply to take the head off, then sew it back to the body in front of the neck. This type of a head provides a flat surface for the face, which is suitable for dollmakers who like to apply paint or appliqué.

ABOVE: *Nigerian Madonna and Child* by Lawan Angelique; 14", cotton knit. Photo by Christina Florkowski.

UPPER RIGHT: *The Quilters* by elinor peace bailey; 24" x 24", cotton. Photo by Isaac Bailey.

LOWER RIGHT: *Frida Kahlo* by Virginia Robertson; 18", cloth. Photo by Virginia Robertson.

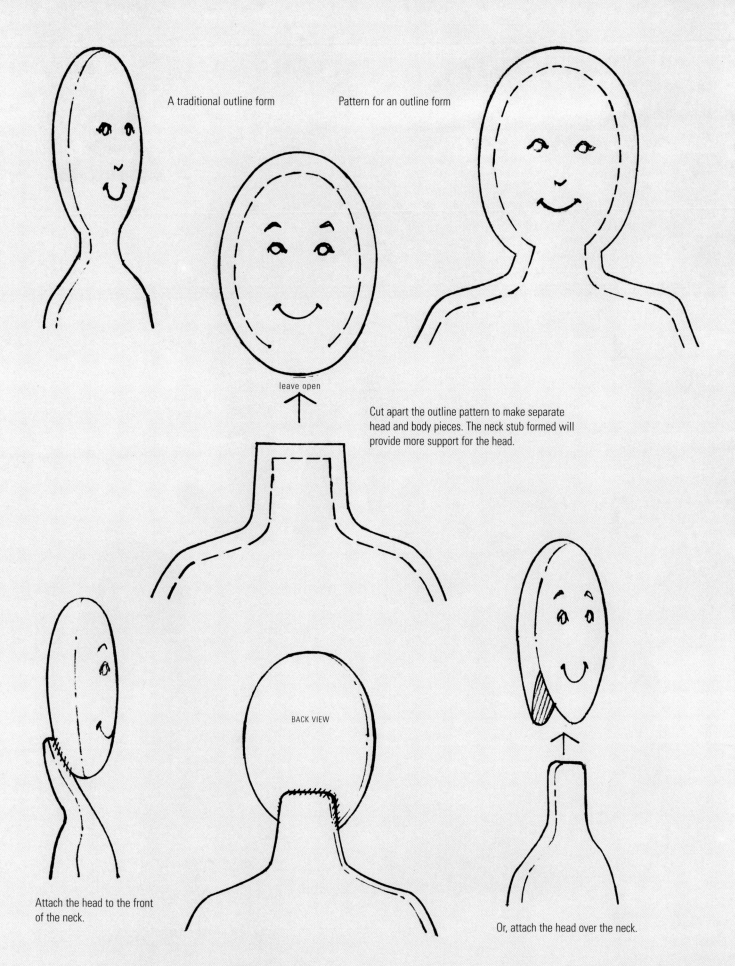

A traditional outline form

Pattern for an outline form

leave open

Cut apart the outline pattern to make separate head and body pieces. The neck stub formed will provide more support for the head.

BACK VIEW

Attach the head to the front of the neck.

Or, attach the head over the neck.

Turns and Curves

To add more dimension or more realism, dollmakers often play with the pattern designs. For example, a dollmaker can change the head pattern so the seam runs down the front of the face. Since the head seam is now 90° away from the shoulder seam, the head and body pieces cannot be sewn together as one piece. The head then becomes a separately attached form. Also, with the head seam running down the front of the face, the front can be curved outward to form a nose. The back could be divided into two curved pieces to give the head even more dimension. Now the dollmaker has a round head with a nose and a chin. You can see from the sketches just how much scope for character development can be had by changing the shapes of the head pieces.

Molly by Joyce Patterson; 16", cloth. Photo by Joyce Patterson.

Maggie McQuire by Bonnie Hoover; 21", cloth. Photo by Scott Hoover.

Go Ahead by Kate Fiebing; 24", cotton. Photo by Les Bricker.

Look Familiar (A Self-Portrait) by Katheryn Tidwell-Foutz; 24", fabric over wire armature. Photo by Les Bricker.

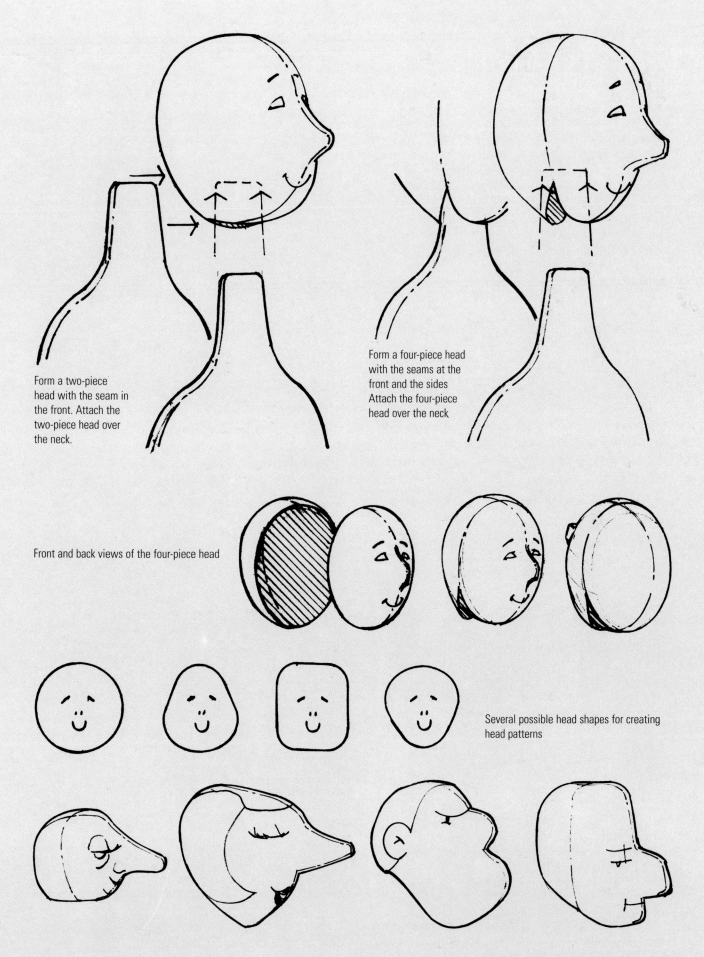

Form a two-piece head with the seam in the front. Attach the two-piece head over the neck.

Form a four-piece head with the seams at the front and the sides Attach the four-piece head over the neck

Front and back views of the four-piece head

Several possible head shapes for creating head patterns

Darts and Contours

Dollmakers often have to choose which contour of the body they want to follow. The contoured head, often called the seamed baseball head, is a common shape that was very popular in the construction of play dolls from the 1930s to the 1970s. The head is constructed of two pieces that form a curved center front. Once the side and front pieces are sewn, the head gets width at the cheek when stuffed. If you want to make a chubby cheeked doll, try this method of head construction.

If you want a round head without a seam in the center front, cut a pattern with a dart. To keep the form rounded, the dart must follow a curved line at the chin. The dart must also be sewn so that it develops smoothly into a point. Separating the head from the neck provides depth and the illusion of cheeks.

A more adult face, one that is longer and not so rounded, requires a pattern that gives chin depth, but no cheek width. Adding a gusset, or inserted pattern piece, spreads the two sides of the face and still maintains a nice shape. The chin gusset can be extended to become part of the front body pattern, either carried down to the bust or waist line, or to the full body front.

Modella-models of a pattern by Susanna Oroyan; 20", cloth. Photo by Don Smith.

The Men's Club by Sally Lampi; 14" to 17", cloth. Photo by Sally Lampi.

Zellnora by elinor peace bailey; 24", cloth. Photo by Don Smith.

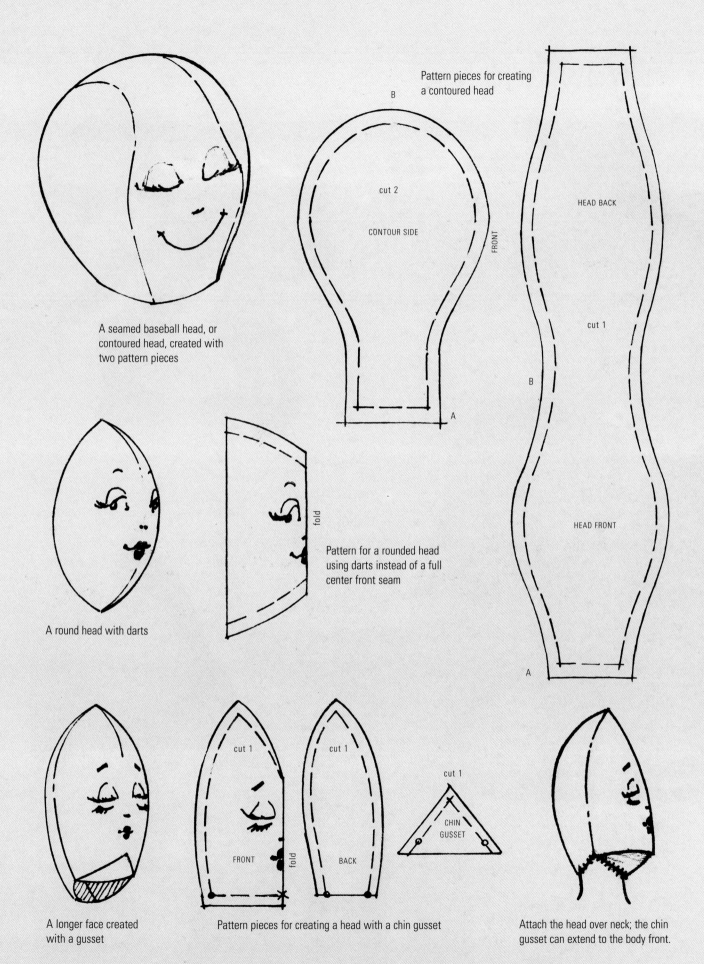

Pattern pieces for creating a contoured head

B

cut 2

CONTOUR SIDE

FRONT

A

HEAD BACK

cut 1

B

HEAD FRONT

A

A seamed baseball head, or contoured head, created with two pattern pieces

A round head with darts

fold

Pattern for a rounded head using darts instead of a full center front seam

A longer face created with a gusset

cut 1

FRONT

fold

cut 1

BACK

cut 1

CHIN GUSSET

Pattern pieces for creating a head with a chin gusset

Attach the head over neck; the chin gusset can extend to the body front.

DARTS AND CONTOURS   33

Fully Sculptural

The fully sculptural head is often used to create needlesculpted and built-up, cloth-covered faces. This variation makes a smoother join with the neck and, if the neck is reinforced with wire armature, a very firmly seated head. To create the head, first construct a two-piece head front (which may or may not have a nose) by sewing entirely around the circumference of two circles. Cut a hole in the back, then turn and stuff the head through the hole. Cut two head back pattern pieces. Sew the head back pieces together, then pin the head front to the back. Handstitch to secure the head, leaving an opening at the center bottom of the head. A neatly seamed head is now formed that can be very securely stitched to the neck.

Knights by Virginia Black; 13", cloth over wire armature. Photo by Virginia Black.

The Sandman by Marlene Denn; detail, cloth. Photo by Les Bricker.

Island Exotica by Susanna Oroyan; 15", cloth over wire armature. Photo by Susanna Oroyan.

Sara Goings by Ellen Turner; 30", cloth. Photo by Anne Hawthorne.

Making Valentines by Lesley Riley; 8" seated, cloth. Photo by Lesley Riley.

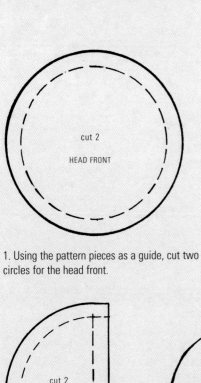

cut 2

HEAD FRONT

1. Using the pattern pieces as a guide, cut two circles for the head front.

2. Sew the head front pieces together, then turn and stuff through a hole cut in one piece.

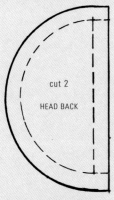

cut 2

HEAD BACK

3. Cut two head back pattern pieces.

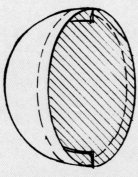

4. Sew the head back pattern pieces together and turn.

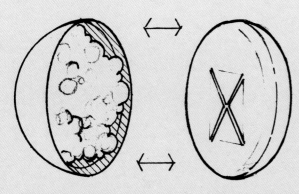

5. Stuff and turn under the edge of the head back piece. Stitch to the head front piece, leaving an opening at the center bottom for the neck.

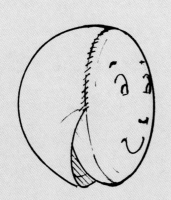

The fully sculptured head without a nose

The fully sculptured head with a nose

Appliquéd Features

Just as a dollmaker begins with flat figures and adapts dimensional techniques, such as jointing and contouring, to express form in space, the same dollmaker can express more realism or character in facial features by adding dimension. Applying or appliquéing another piece of fabric on top of the basic form is the simplest way to add dimension to the flat body. You can think of this method as patching. Pieces are added with hand or machine stitching, or by using glue or fusible iron-on materials. Appliquéd, or patched, features may be flat or they may be padded to add even more height. The patched piece may itself be contoured with darts or gathered to create additional dimension.

Almost any body part or feature can be accentuated by appliqué methods. Usually, the knees, elbows, bust, ears, and sometimes even fingers and toes are added to the body. Noses, eyelids, mouths, and sometimes wrinkles are added to the face. Take your pick—mix and match!

Dumbdolly by Susanna Oroyan; 30", felt. Photo by Don Smith.

Flapper by Barbara Evans; 22", felt. Photo by Barbara Evans.

Harriet by Tracy Page Stillwell; 20", cloth with felt appliqué. Photo by Don Smith.

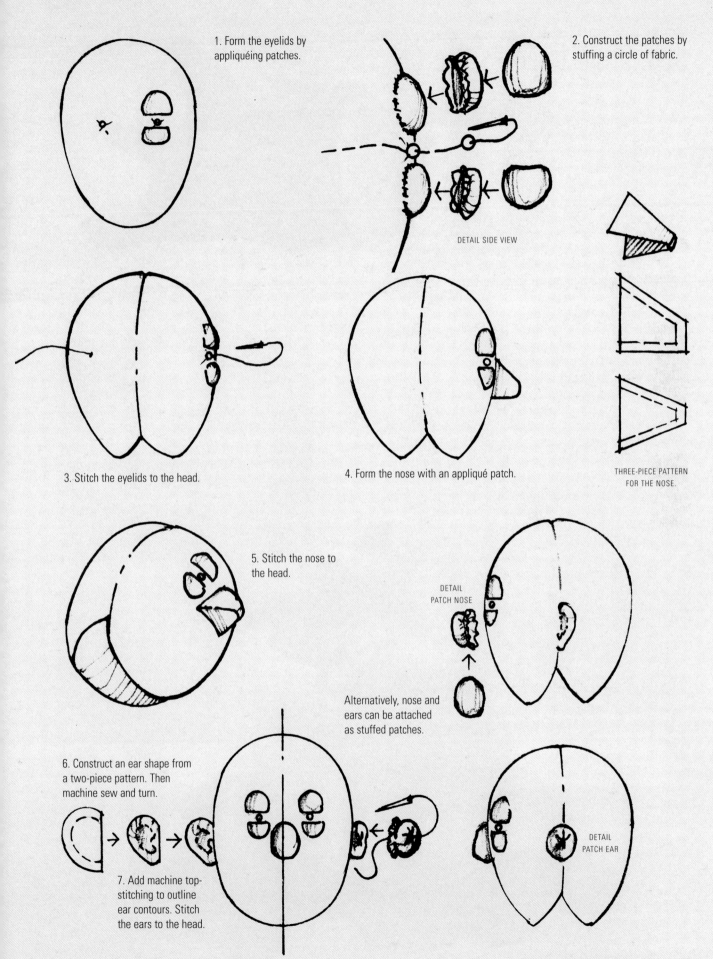

1. Form the eyelids by appliquéing patches.

2. Construct the patches by stuffing a circle of fabric.

DETAIL SIDE VIEW

THREE-PIECE PATTERN FOR THE NOSE.

3. Stitch the eyelids to the head.

4. Form the nose with an appliqué patch.

5. Stitch the nose to the head.

DETAIL PATCH NOSE

Alternatively, nose and ears can be attached as stuffed patches.

6. Construct an ear shape from a two-piece pattern. Then machine sew and turn.

7. Add machine top-stitching to outline ear contours. Stitch the ears to the head.

DETAIL PATCH EAR

Beginning Needlesculpture

Needlesculpture is creating raised sculptural features, such as noses, by stitching the surface fabric to the inner stuffing so that the raised parts will be outlined and secured. Basically, two things happen when you make a doll of woven cloth filled with cotton or polyester stuffing. The first is that the stuffing moves, or can be moved, under the body surface fabric. The second is that the surface fabric stretches as the interior is packed with stuffing.

One problem when making a flat or contoured doll is overcoming the lumps and shifting stuffing so the doll looks smooth and well finished. However, this "problem" can be put to use in needlesculpted dolls. Specifically, one can create raised features if a bump is created in a desired place, such as the nose area, then fixed in place. It might be helpful to think of needlesculpture as quilting, except that not all the stitches go through to the backing fabric layer.

Needlesculpture falls into three categories. The first involves securing a covering over an existing underlayment simple form such as a stuffed head. Essentially, the dollmaker is adding tacking stitches in places that will delineate features. (This method is shown in the illustrations.) The second is the "poke, pick, and stitch to secure," or direct method, which is sculpting a stuffed head without a covering. The third is often called the enhanced underlayment, where extra pads of stuffing material are used to build up the features underneath the covering. Depending on the stitch choices and fabrics, a wide variety of looks can be created. Because needlesculpture has many facets, anyone who has ever held a needle, and many who have not, are attracted to experimenting with needlesculpture.

Sea Bag by Sally Lampi; 5", needlesculpted nylon. Photo by Sally Lampi.

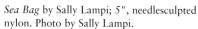

The Blue Elf by Bonnie Boots; 13", needlesculpted nylon. Photo by Bonnie Boots.

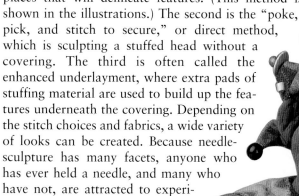

The Birthday Girl by Lawan Angelique; 15" seated, needlesculpted cotton knit. Photo by Christina Florkowski.

Simple Form Needlesculpting

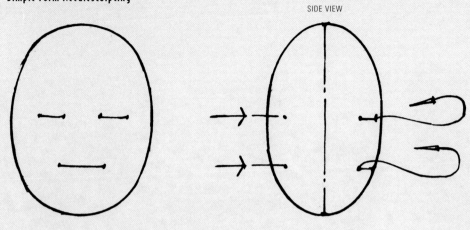

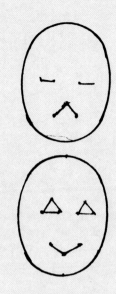

Stitch from the back of the head to define the eyes and mouth area.

Very simple expressions can be made by tacking long stitches.

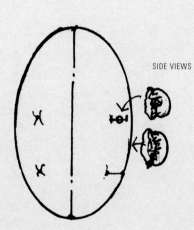

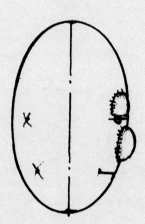

Add more definition by stitching or gluing small wads of stuffing to the face to form eyelids, cheeks, noses, and chins.

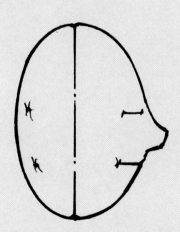

Tack a layer of loosely woven fabric to the sculpted head, to keep the stitches nearly invisible.

Paint or embroider the facial features.

Beginning Stitches

Any fabric can be needle-sculpted, although most dollmakers prefer a medium-to loose-weave cotton or a stretchy fabric. Swimsuit and lingerie fabrics, cotton knits, and nylon stockings are the most commonly used materials. What makes the difference in effect is the choice of fabric. For instance, if the stitches are made on a stuffed ball of nylon stocking mater-ial for a soft head, two or three times as much material needs to be gath-ered, which gives a very bulgy or cartoon-like effect. If the same stitches are made on stuffed woven cotton for a head, it will be more difficult to "pick" or "poke" up a large amount of surface; therefore, the result will be a more con-trolled look. To get the bulgy look, needlesculpt a rough form, then cover the face with a second layer of light, stretchy fabric and tack down with very small, hidden stitches. Since surface stitching shows very little, a highly sculptural effect is achieved with a nice smooth look.

Because needlesculpture requires the doll-maker to be able to put tension on both the thread and fabric, most needlesculpting is done with a double-threaded needle. In most cases common sewing weight thread will suffice; however, for larger areas or for heavyweight fabrics, a dual-duty weight thread might be more advisable. Needlesculpting also requires the dollmaker to stitch through anywhere from less than an inch to over six inches of fabric and stuffing, which requires using a longer, stronger needle. (Needles specially created for doll needle-sculpting are found at craft or sewing suppliers. An option is to use a milliner's needle.) Achieving success with needlesculpture comes with experimentation. The best way to learn it is to try—again and again.

Designer of the Sunrise by Margery Cannon; 19", needlesculpted nylon. Photo courtesy of Margery Cannon.

May 8, 1945 by Doree Pitkin; 24", needle-sculpted cotton. Photo by Les Bricker.

Girl with Ball by Junko Leisfeld; 14", cloth. Photo by John Saxman.

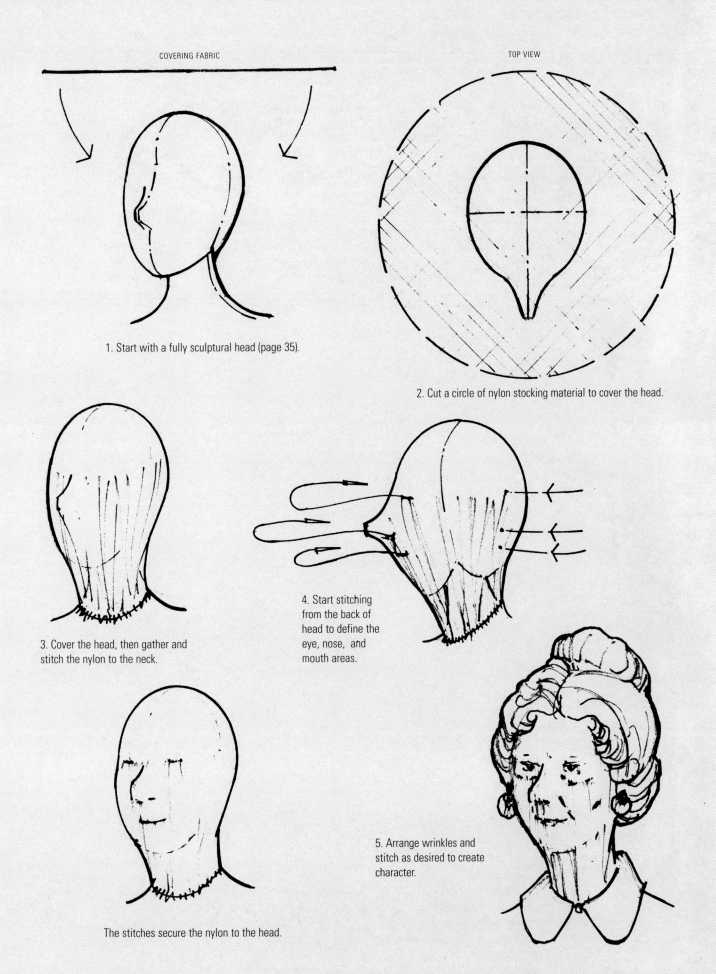

1. Start with a fully sculptural head (page 35).

2. Cut a circle of nylon stocking material to cover the head.

3. Cover the head, then gather and stitch the nylon to the neck.

4. Start stitching from the back of head to define the eye, nose, and mouth areas.

The stitches secure the nylon to the head.

5. Arrange wrinkles and stitch as desired to create character.

Typical Stitch Patterns

The dot indicates where the thread comes out of (or goes into) the back of the head, or the underlayment, to the surface. The line indicates a long stitch that is pulled slightly to form a depression, or gathered to form large areas.

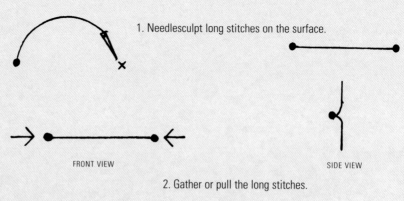

1. Needlesculpt long stitches on the surface.

FRONT VIEW

SIDE VIEW

2. Gather or pull the long stitches.

FRONT VIEW

SIDE VIEW

Flesh puffs are where fabric and stuffing is poked or pulled with the point of the needle to form a mound (puff).

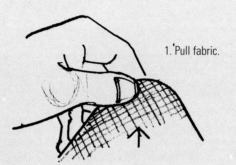

1. Pull fabric.

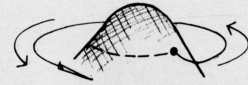

2. Stitch around puff.

3. Pull thread to form a high, rounded shape.

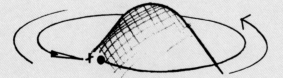

4. Or simply loop thread around raised area.

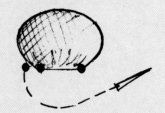

Subsurface needlesculpting (see photo at right) is where thread is run in a zigzag from point to point while taking up a small amount of the underlaying padding.

SUBSURFACE STITCH

Needlesculpture Stitches

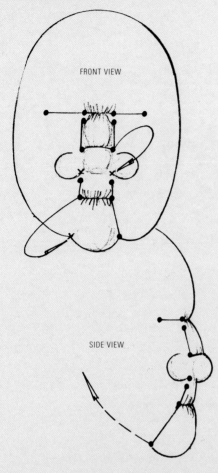

FRONT VIEW

SIDE VIEW

Lady with a Parrot by Jane Darin; 21", cotton knit.
Photo by Joe Darin.

Lady in the Forest by Jane Darin;
21", cotton knit. Photo by Joe Darin.

Male Angel by Jane Darin;
15", cotton knit. Photo by
Joe Darin.

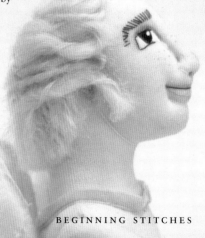

Typical Stitch Patterns

These needlesculpted stitches are "puffier" and show the result of sculpting a very soft, loosely woven fabric such as nylon stocking.

Eyes

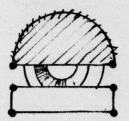

Lay a long stitch between the dots.

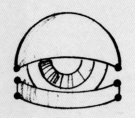

Stitch to bring the ends together.

SIDE VIEW

"Bag ridges" can be substitched (page 42) for more definition and more exact placement.

Puff mouth

Form lips with a series of puffs.

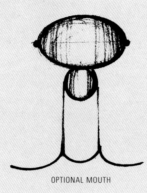

OPTIONAL MOUTH

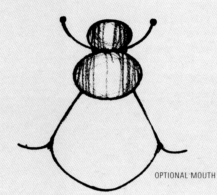

OPTIONAL MOUTH

Straight mouth

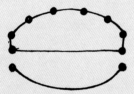

Stitch at dots and gather, then lay thread in center to define upper and lower lips.

Increase tension on center thread to create full mouth.

Define cheek/jowl by bringing the thread in at the inside eye, then lay along the face and under the chin.

Alternative straight mouth

Stitch at dots and pull to gather. Then lay thread in center to define upper and lower lips.

Stitch to form mouth. If desired, pull apart lips to form open mouth.

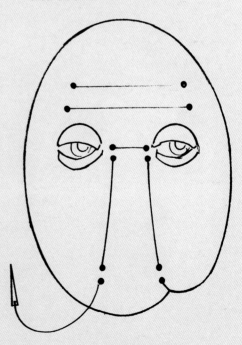

Meara of the Deep by Fayette Knoop;
22", needlesculpted cotton knit.
Photo by Les Bricker.

Tea Ladies by Sally Lampi; 14" to 17", cloth.
Photo by Sally Lampi.

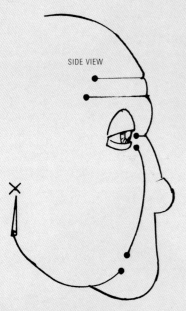

SIDE VIEW

Pull to form cheek/chin and secure
thread at back of head.

Comical Folk Dancer by Toyoko Matsubara; 15", cloth,
needlesculpture. Photo courtesy of Junko Liesfeld.

Direct Needlesculpture

The following stitches show what might happen when a medium-weight woven cotton is needlesculpted. The result is a tighter or controlled look. Varying the amount of stuffing will also make a difference in the final result.

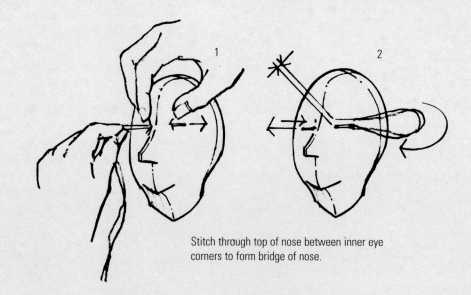

Stitch through top of nose between inner eye corners to form bridge of nose.

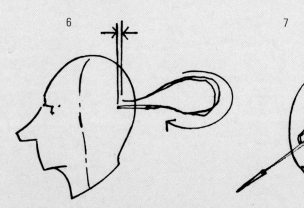

Stitch from outside eye corner to back of head to complete definition of eye area.

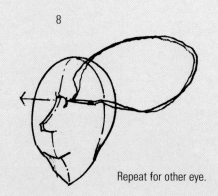

Repeat for other eye.

Let Heaven and Nature Howl by Kathryn Belzer; 17", stuffed cotton. Photo by Danny Abriel.

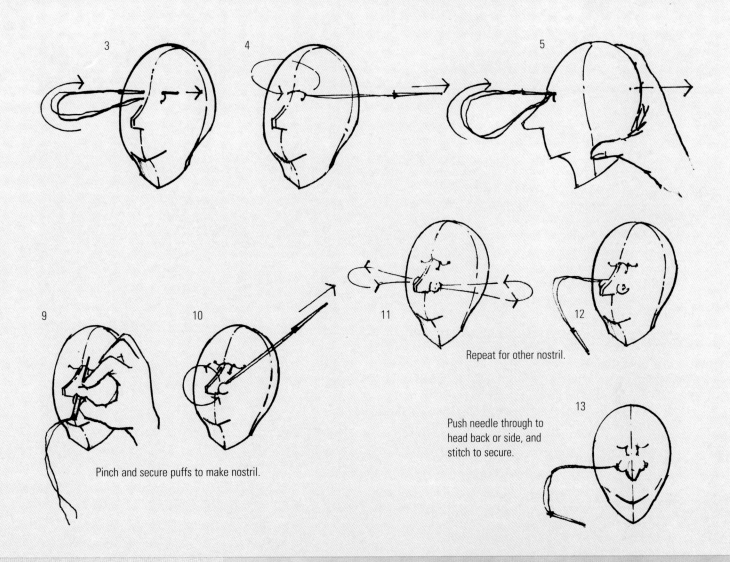

3 4 5

9 10 11 Repeat for other nostril.

12

Pinch and secure puffs to make nostril.

Push needle through to head back or side, and stitch to secure.

13

A Butterfly Collector in Disguise by Sally Lampi; 13½", needlesculpted nylon. Photo by Les Bricker.

Herero Woman in Tribal Costume by Mary Thomas; 14", cloth, needlesculpted and painted face. Photo by Mona Earland.

Beginning to Sculpt

Use any of the head construction methods shown previously as a base to make what we call a built-up head. If a little needlesculpture and a little clay sculpture are combined and covered with cloth, a smooth face surface is made that has a suggestion of real features. This type of head provides a very easy way for cloth dollmakers to begin realistic sculpture.

With the advent of paperclay products (Creative Paperclay™, LaDoll) artists making cloth dolls with painted surfaces started covering the fabric surface of the head with a light layer of paperclay to make a smooth, sandable painting surface. Once they added a bit here and a bit there, noses and chins began to appear. (As they worked, the "wheels" started turning; soon they thought, If I can do this with a head, I could probably solve the problem of flat fabric fingers if I sculpted a layer of paperclay over them!) In order to hide seams on a face that will be painted, dampen paperclay until it forms a mushy paste. Apply paperclay in thin coats with a brush, letting the layer become almost dry between coats. To add eyes to the face, glue on glass or plastic eyes before covering the head with either paperclay or a second layer of cloth. If using cloth, slit the fabric first and work it around the eyes to create eyelids. You can achieve a similar effect by building up the surface with artist's modeling paste or gesso (these products are usually found where artist's oil paints are sold).

However, without a fabric cover, once all the clay and paint materials are applied it is questionable whether the figure is truly a cloth doll. (We generally define the type of doll by the visible surface material.) But lines and boundaries are only imposed by those who are afraid to go over them. Fortunately, in the doll world we have many free spirits who are quite willing to ignore the rules, step over the lines, and adapt whatever techniques and materials seem necessary in order to get the results their imaginations require.

Hannah's Angel by Jacqueline Casey; 18", a light coating of paperclay was used to smooth the surface for painting. Photo by Jaqueline Casey.

Ian and Colin by Rebecca Swanson; 14", a heavier coating of paperclay used under the painted surface. Photo by Rebecca Swanson.

Queen Victoria by Jacqueline Casey; 20",
cloth. Photo by Jacqueline Casey.

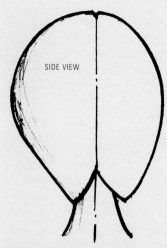

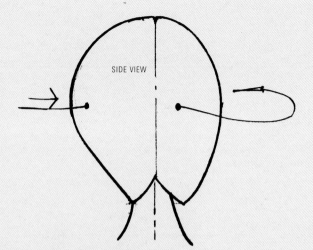

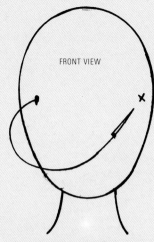

If the head is to be fully covered with fabric, it is necessary to stuff the cloth head very firmly (so no denting can occur).

Stitch from the back of the head to the outside corner of the eye.

Lay the thread across the face, and then stitch to back of head at the other eye corner.

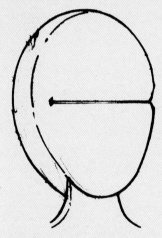

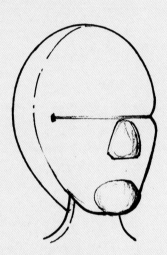

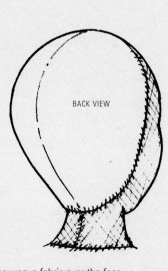

Stitching at the eyeline creates the eye depression and forehead definition.

Build clay to a depth of ⅛" over the face, and then blend to the fabric. Add paperclay to form nose, chin, or facial contours. After the paperclay has dried, apply a light coating of glue to the face.

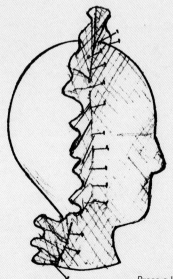

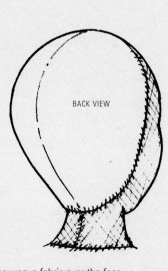

Press a loose weave fabric over the face. Then pin and stitch to the head.

Pressed Cloth

The "So-Easy-It's Ridiculous" method, or, the "Anyone Can Do It" doll head.

Try this technique first; it shows in basic form all the things you will be doing when making more complex forms. In addition to building the basic form head with Styrofoam®, you could also use it as an armature for making paperclay or papier mâché sculpted heads. Simply build the material around the head to a ¼" thickness, leaving a hole for the neck. Let dry, then hollow the Styrofoam interior with a melon-baller or narrow-bladed knife just enough to allow for attaching the neck stub. Try two or three just for fun.

My Little Angel by Jeanie Bates; detail, cloth. Photo by William Sean Sullivan.

Amidia by Joyce Sawyer; 21", cloth. Photo by Les Bricker.

Natalie by Terry Irick; 30", cloth. Photo by Ute Compton.

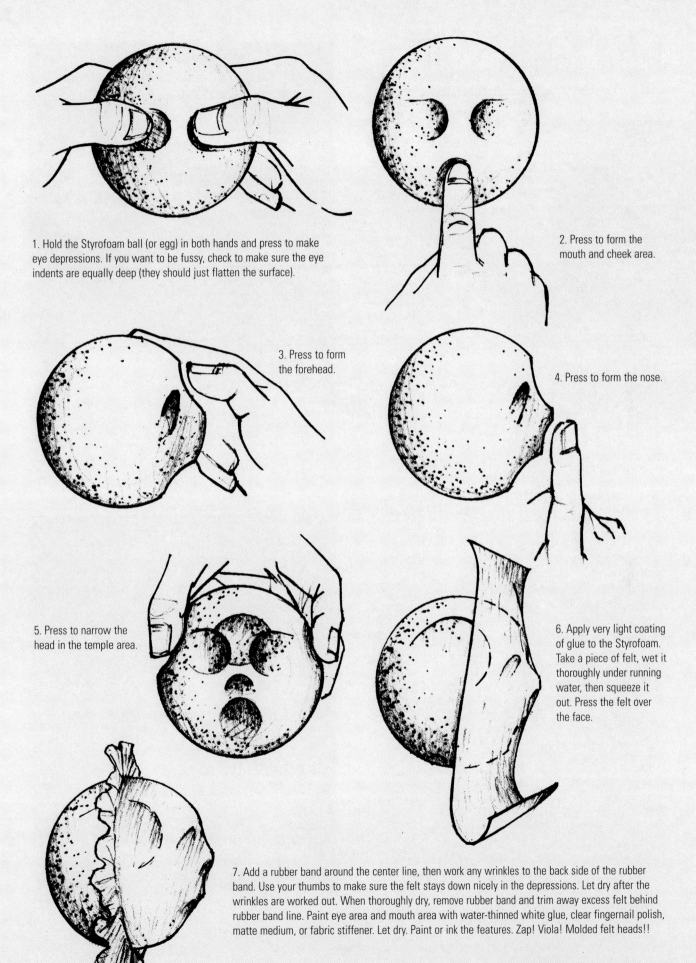

1. Hold the Styrofoam ball (or egg) in both hands and press to make eye depressions. If you want to be fussy, check to make sure the eye indents are equally deep (they should just flatten the surface).

2. Press to form the mouth and cheek area.

3. Press to form the forehead.

4. Press to form the nose.

5. Press to narrow the head in the temple area.

6. Apply very light coating of glue to the Styrofoam. Take a piece of felt, wet it thoroughly under running water, then squeeze it out. Press the felt over the face.

7. Add a rubber band around the center line, then work any wrinkles to the back side of the rubber band. Use your thumbs to make sure the felt stays down nicely in the depressions. Let dry after the wrinkles are worked out. When thoroughly dry, remove rubber band and trim away excess felt behind rubber band line. Paint eye area and mouth area with water-thinned white glue, clear fingernail polish, matte medium, or fabric stiffener. Let dry. Paint or ink the features. Zap! Viola! Molded felt heads!!

Fabric-Covered Sculpture

Oberon's Prize by Carla Thompson; 22" seated, cloth. Photo by Carla Thompson.

Daddy's Home by Carla Thompson; 24" seated, cloth over sculpted face. Photo by Carla Thompson.

The principle of the fabric-covered sculpted head is the same as the simple pressed cloth head (page 50) made by pressing felt over a Styrofoam ball. However, there are two differences.

The first difference is that the artist starts with a sculpted head. Some artists use a model sculpted in soft plasticine clay or a wax head; some use one made of oven-cured polymer-clay, and other artists make molds from their original sculpture and use the mold to cast several heads with poured resin or composition material. If soft clay or wax is used, the result is usually a half head or mask that shows the facial features. The mask fabric is stiffened, then pressed over the hard-sculpted head form. A coating of craft glue or plastic wrap under the fabric allows the mask to release from the original when dry. Once the fabric mask is removed, it is stitched to a stuffed fabric head base. In commercial manufacture, fabric masks are made by steam forming fabric that is sandwiched between metal molds.

The second difference is that the artist must take more care when choosing the fabric for covering the head, which is a bit more painstaking in the application. Whatever the fabric chosen, it must be stretchy or of a fairly loose weave. Cheesecloth, felt, swimsuit knits, stockinette knits, and nylon stocking are possible choices. Since there are more "ups, downs, and corners" in the sculpted head, the artist must work slowly and carefully to work the weave and the bias or stretch of the fabric smoothly over the sculpted features. When the fabric is permanently applied to a cast head, the artist usually applies a very light coating of glue or spray adhesive over the face, then begins working the fabric into place around the nose, the mouth, and the eyes. If a soft clay or fabric form is used, pins can be pushed into the sculpted head to hold the fabric in place until all the parts are in place and the glue is set.

As you look at the dolls shown in this book, you will certainly marvel at some of the lovely pieces that have been made by applying cloth to a sculpted head.

Shella by Carla Thompson; 23", cloth. Photo by Carla Thompson.

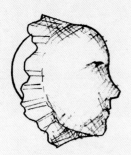

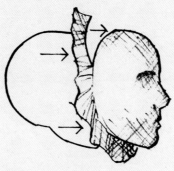

2. Cover the original sculpture with a coating of glue or plastic wrap, then press the stiffener-saturated fabric to the head. Secure with a rubber band.

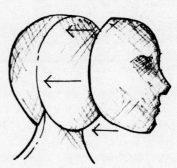

3. Remove the dry mask. Trim and paint.

4. Apply the mask to a fabric head.

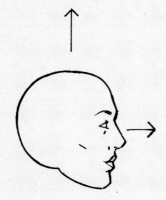

1. Form an original sculpture of hard or soft clay or wax.

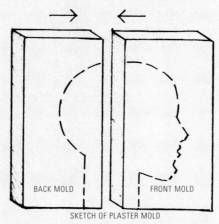

BACK MOLD FRONT MOLD

SKETCH OF PLASTER MOLD

Use mold to cast a head form or to pull an impression.

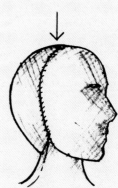

5. Completed face mask.

Method for Pressed Head

1. Press clay material into plaster mold.

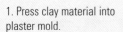

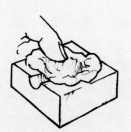

2. Pull impression from mold.

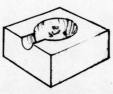

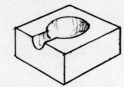

Method for Poured Solid Head

1. Pour resin or liquid composition into mold.

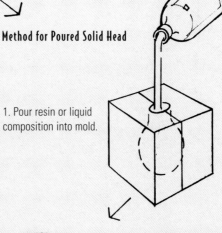

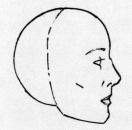

3. Join two halves to make a whole clay head.

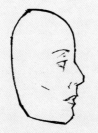

4. Or, half can be used to make mask form.

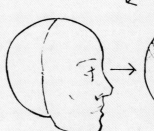

2. Remove solid head from mold.

3. Apply cloth cover to solid head.

Blended Method

Lisa Lichtenfels' sculpted doll figures are the best representation of the contemporary blended method. Her figures are fixed, immobile sculptures to be looked at and appreciated. Lisa uses totally modern, synthetic manufactured products, such as aluminum alloy wire, polyester stuffing, and resin/polymer fiber-based fabrics, that were not available to dollmakers 100 years ago, or even 40 years ago. The surface represents the perfected layering of padding and needlesculpted detail. To achieve this effect, each figure is built on a jointed wire skeleton covered with layers of stuffing to simulate correct musculature. Altogether, each of Lisa's figures demonstrates almost every technique known to the dollmaker. Some of them even include controls so that eyes and jaws can be moved. It is easy to see this use of material and method, combined with computer chips and fiber optics, very nearly mimicking a living human form in motion.

Although the techniques and processes illustrated in this book are used regularly by a number of dollmakers, Lisa's methods are her own unique refinements of these processes. An attempt by someone else to describe them

Persephone by Lisa L. Lichtenfels; 24", nylon stocking over wire armature. Photo by Lisa L. Lichtenfels.

or teach them from observation could only be superficial at best. In order to complete the discussion of the head construction techniques shown, Lisa has allowed us to excerpt and illustrate her basic approach, which she discusses in her book, *The Basic Head: Soft Sculpture Techniques*. Even in its simplest form, it is not a process for the faint of heart, but it is the one process using fabric and fiber where the results will most likely reflect the anatomical complexities of the human head.

Walyo and her Nephew by Lisa L. Lichtenfels; 27", nylon stocking over wire armature. Photo by Lisa L. Lichtenfels.

Belinda (Woman as Egg) by Lisa L. Lichtenfels; 15", nylon stocking over wire armature. Photo by Lisa L. Lichtenfels.

1. Draw a head to the correct anatomical proportions.

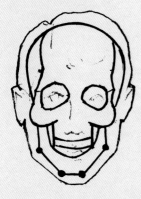

2. Draw the skull over the sketch to locate important points of bone structure.

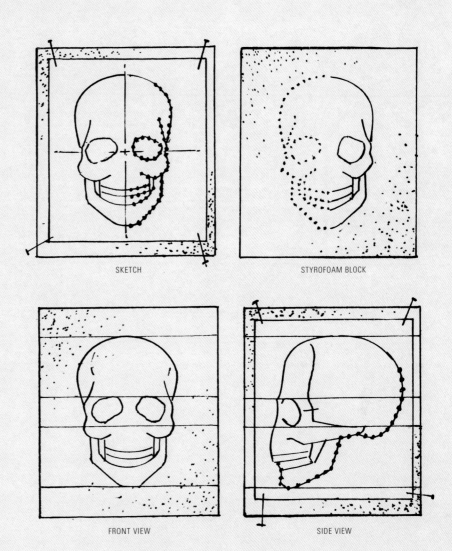

SKETCH   STYROFOAM BLOCK

FRONT VIEW   SIDE VIEW

3. Transfer the skull shape and detail drawings to a Styrofoam block.

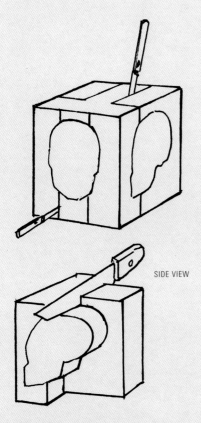

SIDE VIEW

4. Cut away the Styrofoam and carve to form a skull.

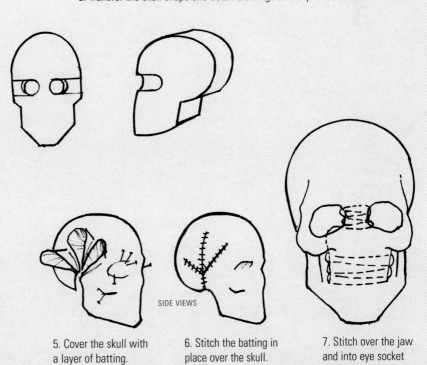

SIDE VIEWS

5. Cover the skull with a layer of batting.

6. Stitch the batting in place over the skull.

7. Stitch over the jaw and into eye socket depressions.

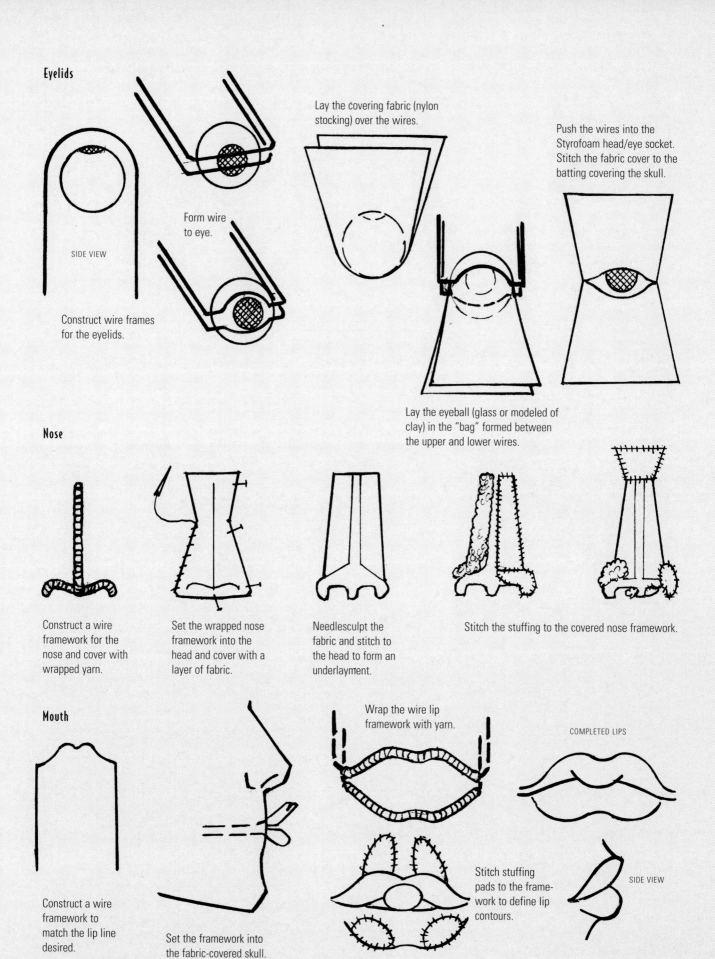

Eyelids

SIDE VIEW

Construct wire frames for the eyelids.

Form wire to eye.

Lay the covering fabric (nylon stocking) over the wires.

Lay the eyeball (glass or modeled of clay) in the "bag" formed between the upper and lower wires.

Push the wires into the Styrofoam head/eye socket. Stitch the fabric cover to the batting covering the skull.

Nose

Construct a wire framework for the nose and cover with wrapped yarn.

Set the wrapped nose framework into the head and cover with a layer of fabric.

Needlesculpt the fabric and stitch to the head to form an underlayment.

Stitch the stuffing to the covered nose framework.

Mouth

Construct a wire framework to match the lip line desired.

Set the framework into the fabric-covered skull.

Wrap the wire lip framework with yarn.

Stitch stuffing pads to the framework to define lip contours.

COMPLETED LIPS

SIDE VIEW

Adding Soft Tissue

Form the soft tissues of the face after the feature framework and base padding is added. The older face will require more padded areas in order to provide the lines and contours of aging skin.

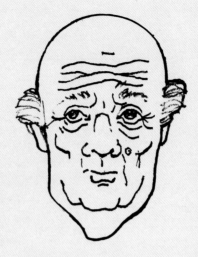

Finishing the head consists of pinning the "skin" fabric in place over the padded base. The stitches are run from the back of the head and sides of the skull, through or under the base padding, to secure the nylon around the framed and padded features.

Stitching the Eye Area

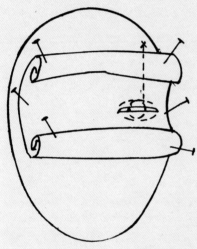

A final "skin" of nylon stocking fabric is laid over the face. The fabric is slit to allow the eyes to show.

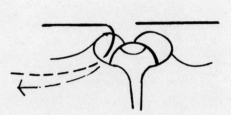

Variation: Instead of constructing an eye "bag" the cut edge of the top/skin layer is brought under eyeball/lid framework.

Secure the edges with stitches running from the socket to the back and sides of the head.

Stitching the Nose Area

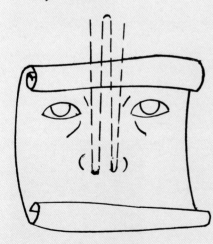

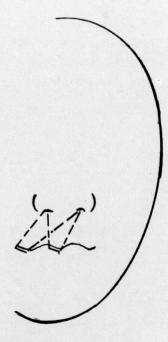

When needlesculpting, all the stitching is done so that the surface is tacked as invisibly as possible to the underlayment.

Rolling the "skin" fabric as the stitches are placed enables working from the back and protecting the surface from possible snagging.

Subsurface stitching to secure upper lip.

Masks

The Chess Players by Akira Blount; 16" x 24", needle-sculpted, gesso and fabric painted masks. When raised, the mask on each figure forms a hat that is an integral part of the figure's image. Photo by David Luttrel.

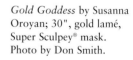

The external mask is a transitional step between the all-fabric figures and mixed-media figures. In many cultures the mask allows an ordinary human actor the ability to portray a spirit, a god, or a supernatural figure. Creating a doll with a mask adds to the dimension of character an artist can show. It also adds an element of mystery—what or who is under the mask?

A mask can be made of any material. Masks made for fabric figures usually are sculpted or modeled of oven-curing or air-drying clay. Sometimes they are shaped by pressing fabric saturated with a stiffener over a clay or fabric model. This allows the fiber artist to play with another medium of expression. The mask can be carried by the figure or attached to the head with a string, ribbon, or rubber band. Or the mask could be hand carried in the traditional wearing modes, or hinged or sewn to the head...or, think of a unique method of attachment for your own pieces.

Trickster by Peggy Flynn; 12", ceramic mask on fabric, raffia hair. Photo by Mark Carleton.

Gold Goddess by Susanna Oroyan; 30", gold lamé, Super Sculpey® mask. Photo by Don Smith.

Monkey Masks by Andra Dunn; 19" seated, papier mâché on velveteen. As Andra Dunn sees it, a mask is an element of how the figure itself wants to express its personality. Photos by Andra Dunn.

Method I

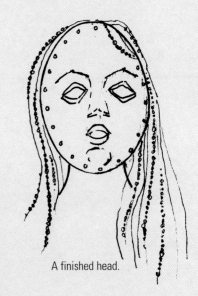

Make a ¼" thick pancake of air-drying or oven-curing clay. With a toothpick or modeling tool, sketch a simple face, then poke sew holes around edges.

Cure or dry the mask, paint as desired, and stitch to cloth face.

A finished head.

Method II

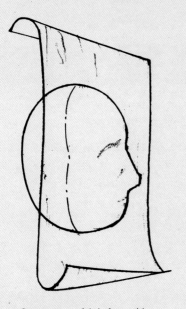
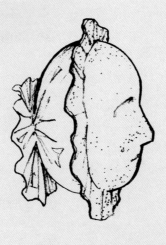

Cover a sewn fabric face with kitchen plastic wrap.

Over the plastic wrap, apply fabric saturated in fabric stiffener, then smooth the wrinkles to the back.

Let the mask dry. Lift it away from the head. Holes may be cut for the eyes and mouth. Beads, or plastic or glass eyes may be inserted, or clay can be added for more sculpture.

Method III

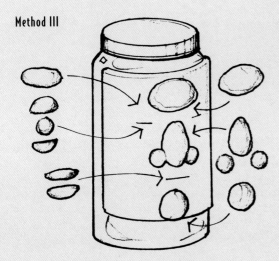

On a rounded, smooth surface, such as a jar or can, apply air-drying or oven-curing clay.

Model the simple mask form. Smooth, blend, and trim to desired facial form.

Slightly loosen the mask from the jar surface so it can be removed easily after curing. Air dry, or cure in oven, using the jar or can to hold the form.

Painting

There is no doubt that one of the attractions to doll-making is that it is an art that allows the artist to use any and all materials, embellishments, or media techniques. Painting on dolls covers a number of known techniques and any number of applications yet to be discovered by the experimental maker. Almost any coloring medium, from house paint to eyeshadow, can be used on a doll. What follows are two basic "recipes" for painting, with some notes to get you started.

If you have come to dollmaking without prior experience in drawing and painting, the first recommendation is practice. To develop your ability to control the brush, pen, or pencil for the desired effect, practice on scrap fabrics or throw-away doll parts. Drawing and painting on fabric is not the same as working on paper because fabric has nap or fibers which cause drag on the drawing tools. Fabric also has open spaces in the weave which absorb liquid colors and make them bleed beyond a desired line. You will need to know how to control these factors to get a successful coloring on your doll.

The second recommendation is test. Do not apply paints, colors, or sealers you have not tested previously on scrap fabric. Some inks in commercially available pens will bleed on fabrics; some sealers applied to powdery colors, such as chalks and eyeshadows, will cause them to liquefy and run. Know what will happen before you apply colors to the finished doll.

LIGHT BODY PAINT

Use this effect if you want to tint the body or create an illusion of light and shadow by varying the surface color. You will need a large, soft-bristled brush, plus watercolor or acrylic paints, a palette, and a cup of water.

Note: Watercolors from a paintbox will be very light and almost trans-

Woman Warrior by Barbara Buysse; 18", painted cloth. Photo by Don Smith.

parent; watercolors from a tube may be mixed with water to achieve a transparent wash, or opaque effects; and acrylic paints will be heavier and more opaque in effect. When these paints are applied directly, the weave of the fabric, the seams, and the stitches will show after painting.

Application: Begin with a completed, stuffed body. Wet the brush and paint only the water onto the fabric to dampen the surface. When the surface is damp, add color to the brush and paint until a desirable color or color variation is achieved. Remember, the more water used with the paint medium, the more likely the paint will "puddle," so paint quickly, keeping the brush working over the whole surface until the base coats are satisfactory.

HEAVY BODY PAINT

Use this method on woven cloth dolls (muslin, linen) if you want the end result to look like an oil painting, or when the desired result is a smooth glossy surface.

Note: The completed, stuffed body must be primed with gesso and/or a fabric stiffener to create a hard, smooth surface that will receive paint. Priming eliminates much of the surface fiber or fuzz. It also seals the spaces in the weave so

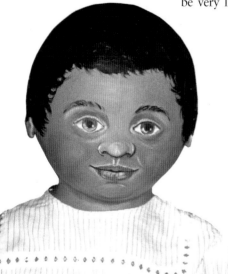

Fairchildren Hattie and Josephine by Helen Pringle; 36", stuffed, oil painted. Photo by T. R. Miller.

that paint will not bleed. You should be aware that a hard-painted surface on a soft stuffed body can dent. Since dents are difficult to fix, the possibilities for denting can be reduced if the body is stuffed very tightly.

Heavy body paints may be applied with any type of brush. You will probably find a wide, medium-bristled brush most compatible for the base body color. A selection of fine- and medium-tipped brushes will be needed for painting facial features.

Priming is done with gesso, or a fabric stiffener may be used. If using the latter, apply the stiffener first, following the directions on the label. Use unthinned acrylics from a jar or tube, artist's oil colors, or latex household paints. Seal the finished painted surfaces, if desired, with matte or gloss sealers used for flat art paintings.

Application: Apply fabric stiffener, if desired, then let dry. Paint on the gesso until the surface is thoroughly covered. Apply as many coats as needed to create the desired surface. If you want the fabric to show through with a canvas effect, or if you want a brushstroke effect, you will need only one or two coats of gesso. Let the gesso dry, then blend and apply body surface colors. Let dry again and apply the features.

Caution: Artist's oil colors, certain dyes, and sealers should not be used on dolls which children may play with. Some paints and sealers are flammable, and many contain toxic chemicals. Always check labels and follow manufacturer's directions for use. Also note that over time and under some atmospheric conditions, painted surfaces can crack and chip. Generally, fully painted surfaces are only used on dolls made as art pieces, primarily for display and, as such, handled minimally. Also note that some clear sealers such as shellac or fingernail polish may yellow over time.

UPPER RIGHT: Head by elinor peace bailey; 4", cloth, colored pens. Photo by Susanna Oroyan.

UPPER LEFT: *Meribeth* by Beverly Port; 20", painted silk. Photo by Don Smith.

LOWER LEFT: *Leslie* by Norma Malerich; 33", painted cloth. Photo by Norma Malerich.

LOWER RIGHT: *Chelsea* by Charlene Westling; 15½", cloth. Photo by Don Smith.

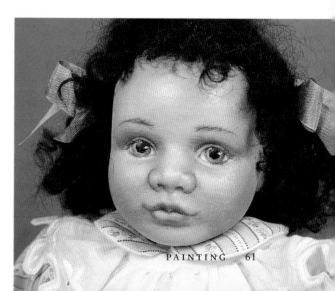

Regina by Rebecca Swanson
14", painted cloth over paperclay
Photo by Rebecca Swanson

Oriental Mermaid by Andra Dunn
17", painted papier mâché
Photo by Andra Dunn.

Pandora by Jacqueline Casey
20", needlesculpted cotton
Photo by Jacqueline Casey.

Yellow Mary by Marcella Welch
4 feet, fabric over sculpted paperclay
Photo by Jerry Anthony.

Courting the Flame by Maggie Mayer
21", painted cloth
Photo by Maggie Mayer.

Sarah Piper by Becky Craver
13½", needlesculpted Lycra
Photo by Becky Craver.

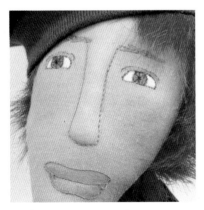

Turtleman Waiting in a Chair
by Deborah Spanton
12", embroidered cotton
Photo by Sherrie Cummins.

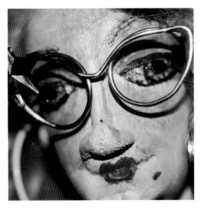

Marlyn Macaroni by Linda Ewing
15", needlesculpted and painted cotton
Photo by Linda Ewing.

Melony by Mary Thomas
18", needlesculpted and painted cloth
Photo by Mona Earland.

Jester by Akiko Anzai
18", paperclay covered with fabric
Photo by Akiko Anzai.

Under the Mask by Dinah Sargeant
25", embroidered and painted cloth
Photo by Dinah Sargeant.

Alyssum by Jeanie Bates
16", knit fabric over sculpted head
Photo by Willian Sean Sullivan.

Aunt Cora by Virginia Robertson
26", needlesculpted cotton
Photo by Don Smith.

Pearl by Barbara Spencer
27", cloth
Photo by Pat Stark.

Love Temple by Pamela Hastings
15", paper, fabric
Photo by David Egan.

Ice Princess by Julie McCullough
22", Lycra® over needlesculpted velour
Photo by John Nollendorfs.

Appliqué Face by Susanna Oroyan
4", felt and embroidery
Photo by Susanna Oroyan.

Helen Hundertwasser by Margi Hennen
10", embroidered cloth
Photo by Warren Dodgson.

The Basic Body

For the creative dollmaker the idea always comes first, then the pattern is created as a way to express the idea. As you look through this book and the many different examples of artist-made dolls, I hope you conclude that the pattern is not so important as the idea. What makes each piece unique is the detailing that the individual creator discovers and develops to express the idea.

The key element throughout the construction process is holding the idea. Let's look at how this might be done. In the works of Antonette (Noni) Cely, we see very realistic-looking lady figures. Their appeal comes as much from the excellent proportion, pose, and form as it does from the beautiful faces and meticulous detail. The basic pattern, however, might appear to you to be quite simple. Surprisingly, most doll patterns are quite simple. The "magic" happens when the artist applies specific details such as needlesculpture, wire armature, and carefully arranged costume draping.

A Slight Adjustment by Antonette Cely; 16", cloth with cloth over Fimo. Noni visualizes the line and form of the pose she has in mind (here the lady reaching to adjust her stocking seam) and at each step makes inventions or decisions to bring that vision to reality. Photo by Don Cely.

Rita by Antonette Cely; 16", cloth with cloth over Fimo®. Photo by Don Cely.

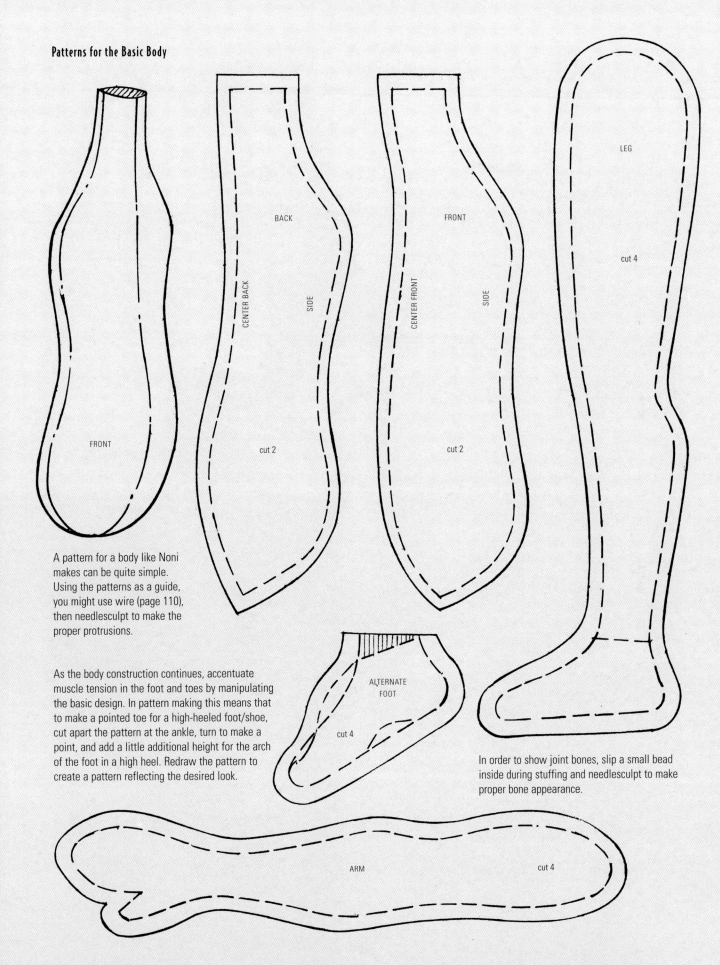

A pattern for a body like Noni makes can be quite simple. Using the patterns as a guide, you might use wire (page 110), then needlesculpt to make the proper protrusions.

As the body construction continues, accentuate muscle tension in the foot and toes by manipulating the basic design. In pattern making this means that to make a pointed toe for a high-heeled foot/shoe, cut apart the pattern at the ankle, turn to make a point, and add a little additional height for the arch of the foot in a high heel. Redraw the pattern to create a pattern reflecting the desired look.

In order to show joint bones, slip a small bead inside during stuffing and needlesculpt to make proper bone appearance.

FRONT

BACK

CENTER BACK

SIDE

cut 2

FRONT

CENTER FRONT

SIDE

cut 2

LEG

cut 4

ALTERNATE FOOT

cut 4

ARM

cut 4

Body Contours

When dollmakers want to show depth with the form, or, essentially, want to show the figure as occupying space dimensionally, they are faced with figuring out how to make two pieces of flat fabric take on specific, rather than generalized volume when stuffed.

There are two typical ways of adding depth or dimension when designing patterns. The first is contouring the patterns, which means designing pattern pieces with curves, so that when the curves are sewn together and stuffed the effect is a rounded figure. The second method is the dressmaker's dart. While contouring usually involves three- or four-part body pieces, the dart can provide depth with just two pieces. In both methods the dollmaker needs to think about and become very aware of the planes of the body, or the "edges" of the form, from various viewpoints.

For instance, if we look at the lower leg from the side it looks as though it has two sides: the straight front, and the back curve that follows the line of the calf muscle. If we look at it from the back, it looks like one triangular piece. The question then is how to achieve both appearances. The answer: a three-piece lower leg pattern, or a dart at the upper back of the calf. To a certain extent careful stuffing of a two-piece outline form will achieve this appearance, but a self-challenged dollmaker often wants the more exact form.

Generic Chess Knight by Nancy Laverick; 16", cotton and Ultrasuede®. Photo by Azad.

Belle by Nancy Laverick; 19", cotton. Photo by Nancy Laverick.

Patterns for the Contoured Body

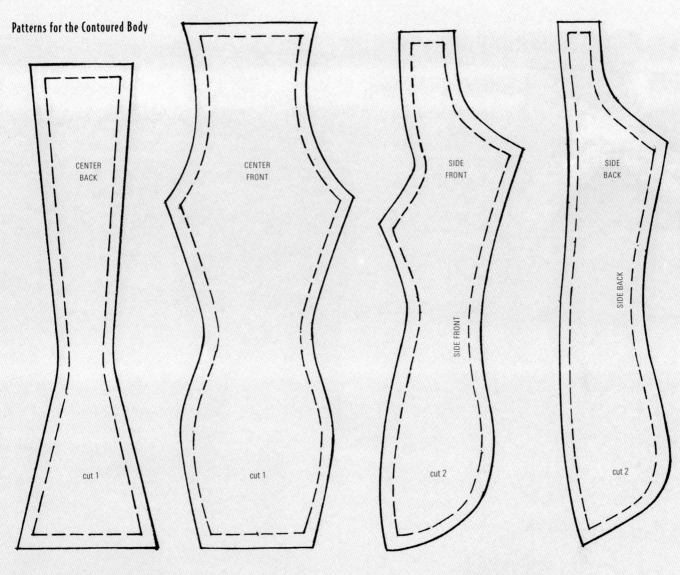

CENTER BACK

cut 1

CENTER FRONT

cut 1

SIDE FRONT

SIDE FRONT

cut 2

SIDE BACK

SIDE BACK

cut 2

Pattern pieces for creating a contoured body; the arm and leg pattern pieces on page 65 may be scaled to fit this body.

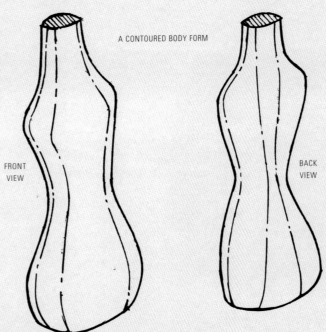

A CONTOURED BODY FORM

FRONT VIEW

BACK VIEW

Traditional Japanese Body

The tradition of dollmaking is ancient and highly respected in Japan. Many of the more complex techniques of Japanese dollmaking require materials not available in other countries. Of course, cloth and wire are universal, so the following method is one that anyone can make and adapt for many effects.

This method, shared by artist Junko Liesfeld, was taught to her by her mother, Toyoko Matsubara and, as you can see, used by her sister, Akiko Sasaki. Do notice how the same technique used by three different artists has developed into three distinct styles or statements for each artist. Another aspect worth noting is that the head is not attached to a neck stub, but is inserted into the body, which is different from most of the forms shown in this book. This is a good example of the choices a designer faces when deciding how to cut parts, where to show seams, and which elements of the body's anatomy to show in detail and how to make them move.

Clown by Akiko Sasaki; 17", cloth. Photo by Akiko Sasaki.

The Accountant by Junko Liesfeld; 14", cloth. Photo by Jeff Saxman.

Grandma by Toyoko Matsubara; 10", cloth. Photo courtesy of Junko Liesfeld.

Heads

A basic head shape

A needlesculpted head

A built-up head

STUFFING

Head Attachment

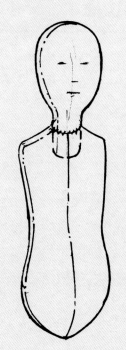

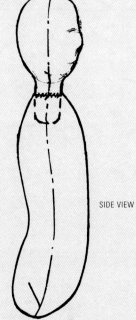

SIDE VIEW

Gather the body around the neck.

Bodies

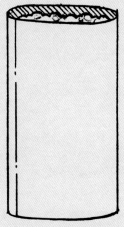

A basic tubular
body shape

BACK

CENTER

A contoured body
with dart

CENTER

FRONT

A contoured body

Legs

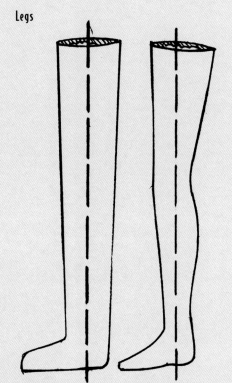

A simple leg form

A contoured leg form

Hands

A simple hand
shape

A complex hand
shape

Posed Body Forms

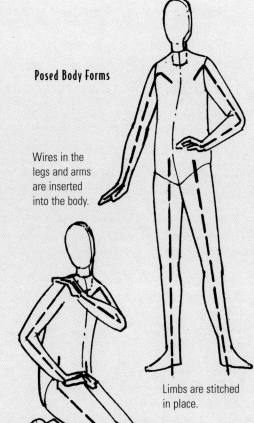

Wires in the
legs and arms
are inserted
into the body.

Limbs are stitched
in place.

Shaping the Bust

Children under the age of eight are usually very accepting of abstract form in a doll. But after their eighth year children become very aware of details and very much want their dolls to look realistic. It becomes important for little girls to have a realistic female form for imaginative play and to dress in correct "grown-up lady" costumes. Little boys want figures that can move to simulate real-life actions. As adults we are attracted to realistic detail in both the anatomy and costuming of a figure.

When designing the bust for realism, the following approaches can be used: the simple appliquéd patch, the darted dress form, the contour, and the undergarment. Many times the choice of type reflects the maker's particular artistic view or need when creating a costume form. The number of possible variations on these methods is apparently endless, and certainly fascinating for the viewer.

Art and Dottie by Deb Shattil; 21", cotton over wire armature. Photo by Kate Cameron.

Art and Dottie back view; note the interesting seaming contour in the trousers.

Venus by Akiko Anzai; 18", cloth, needlesculpted. Photo by Akiko Anzai.

Appliquéd Patch Form

Form the chest with appliquéd patches.

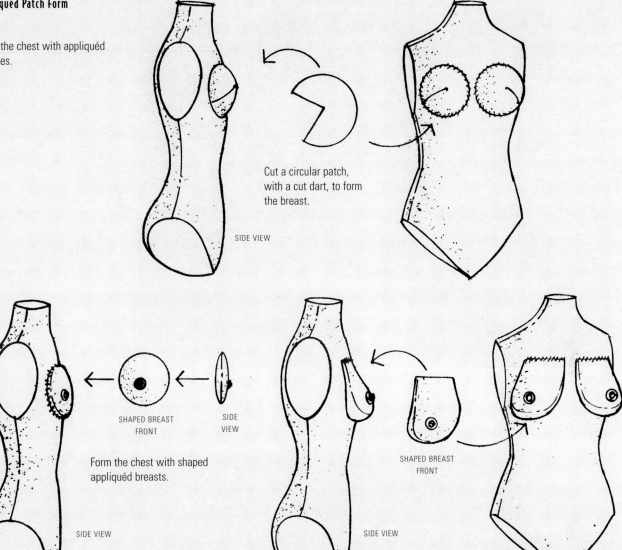

Cut a circular patch, with a cut dart, to form the breast.

SIDE VIEW

Form the chest with shaped appliquéd breasts.

SHAPED BREAST FRONT

SIDE VIEW

SIDE VIEW

SHAPED BREAST FRONT

SIDE VIEW

The Darted Dress Form

Form the chest with darts sewn at the chest area.

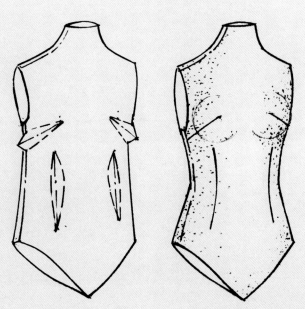

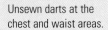

Unsewn darts at the chest and waist areas.

Sewn darts form the bust and contoured waist.

TOP: *Happy Birthday Honey* by Gloria Winer; 15", cloth over wire armature. Photo by Jim Winer.

BOTTOM LEFT: *Aunt Zorah Sunday Morning* by Doree Pitkin; 24", cloth. Photo by Doree Pitkin.

BOTTOM RIGHT: *Ladies in the Steam Bath* by Susanna Oroyan; 12" seated, cloth with Sculpey® masks. Photo by Don Smith.

The Contoured Form

Form the chest with a contoured bust.

BUST TOP

UNDER GUSSET

Sew the bust top and under gusset together, then stuff and stitch to the torso.

Undergarment Forms

Form the chest with a contoured brassiere bust.

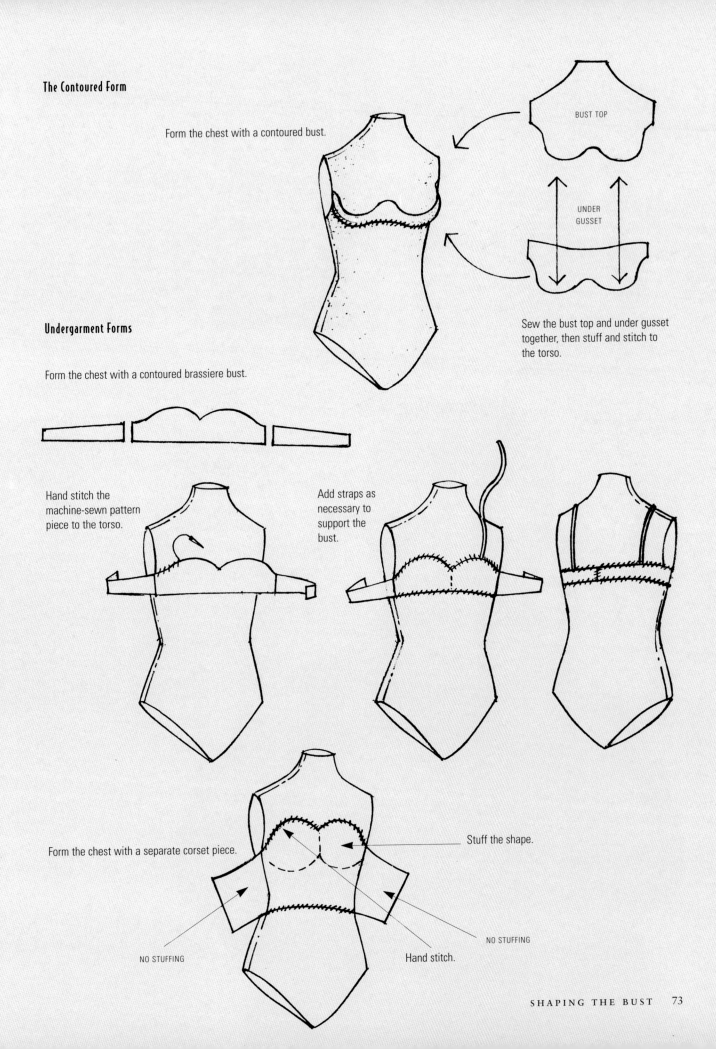

Hand stitch the machine-sewn pattern piece to the torso.

Add straps as necessary to support the bust.

Form the chest with a separate corset piece.

Stuff the shape.

NO STUFFING

NO STUFFING

Hand stitch.

Hands

Because hands and fingers are usually very small shapes, they are a challenge for the dollmaker. Learning to choose the correct form for the piece, and executing it well, will make the piece very dramatic, no matter what type. Usually little skinny fingers and fat palms cause frustration when creating a hand. When the fingers, a very small area of fabric, are stuffed, the stuffing makes them even thinner. The palm has more fabric area, so when it is stuffed it gets fatter. What to do? Take darts in either the hand back or the palm to help even up the proportion of hand to fingers. Also note that a cloth hand may be posed, refined with needlesculpting stitches, and painted so that it will hold its position. Or try to saturate the hand with fabric stiffener or cover with paper-clay to create a hard surface. No matter what form you prefer, a well-executed hand can contribute as much to the success of a piece as the face.

Renaissance Lady and The Meso-American Man by Ellen Rixford; life-sized. The lady is nylon over polyfil, with foam and wire understructure, and the man is sculpted and painted foam. Photo by Ellen Rixford.

Courting the Flame by Maggie Mayer; 21", muslin. Photo by Maggie Mayer.

Invincible Spirit by Charlene Westling; 17" seated, cloth over sculpted form. Photo by Don Smith.

These basic hands adapt well to rag doll and basic doll forms. All of these shapes can be hand sewn or top-stitched to define the fingers.

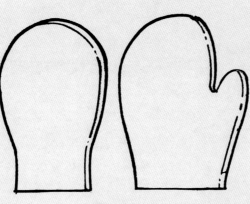

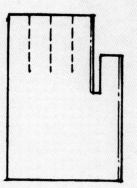 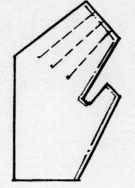

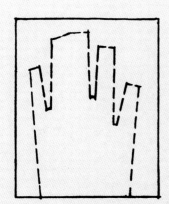 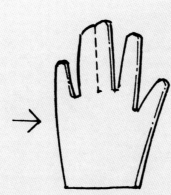

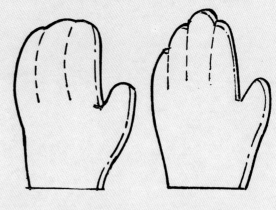

Try a unique hand design that has fingers of rolled and stitched felt.

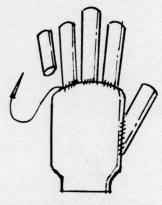

Movable fingers can be made by sewing and stuffing the fingers separately, then hand stitching each one to the stuffed palm.

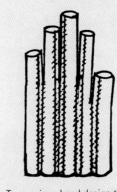

This style of hand works well when using nylon stocking. Note the amount of stretch that occurs in stuffing.

A wire armature may be inserted for the arm.

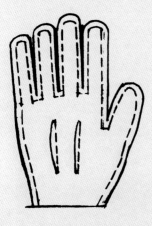 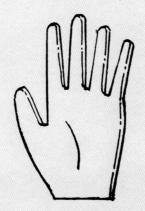 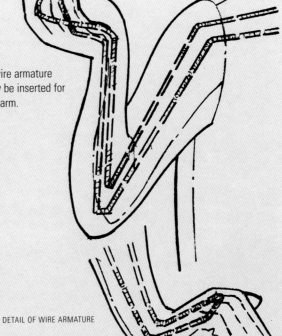

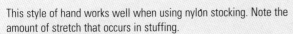

BACK OF HAND   PALM OF HAND   DETAIL OF WIRE ARMATURE

Darts made in the hands before stuffing can make stuffed fingers more proportionate to the hand.

THE POSABLE HAND: METHOD I

If desired, hands can be made separately to "plug" into an arm. These types of hands are frustrating because of the difficulties of turning such small areas of cloth. To ease the process, we show how to use a hollow turning tube. There is also a commercial tube which hooks and pulls the end of the finger. (Some artists like to use the tweezers-like medical hemostat.) You can purchase turning tubes at shops, or they may be adapted from metal tubing, or even drinking straws.

CENTER: *Everything in the World* by Pamela Hastings; 24", muslin. Photo by Allen Bryan.

LOWER LEFT: *Birthday Clown* by Barbara Willis; 18", cloth. Photo by Photomaster.

RIGHT: *Fiddling Angel* by Jacqueline Casey; 18", cloth over wire armature. Photo by Jacqueline Casey.

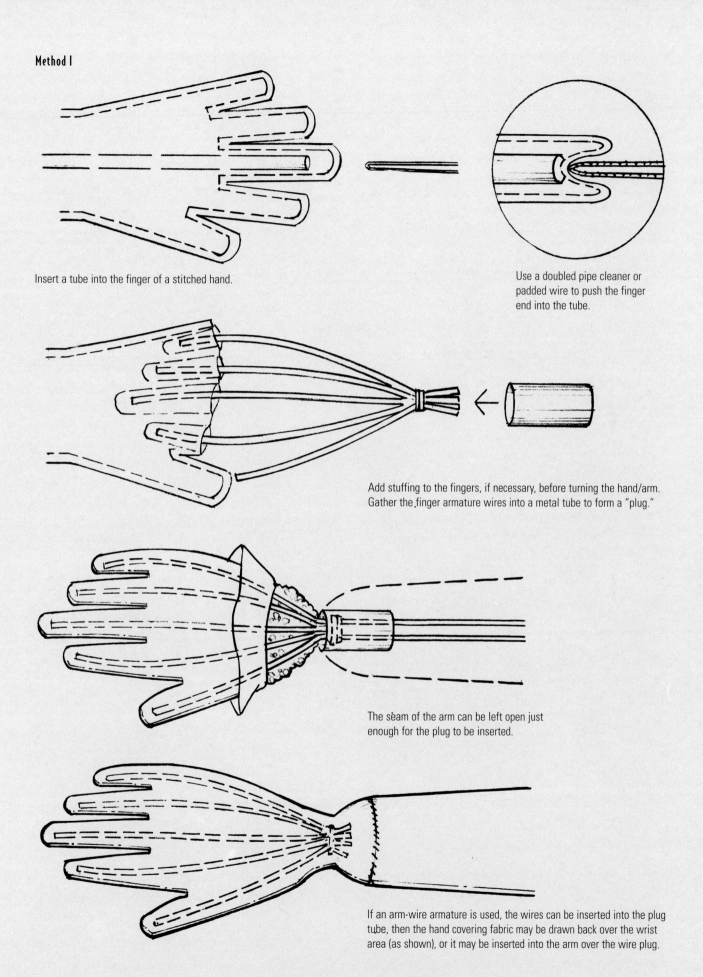

Insert a tube into the finger of a stitched hand.

Use a doubled pipe cleaner or padded wire to push the finger end into the tube.

Add stuffing to the fingers, if necessary, before turning the hand/arm. Gather the finger armature wires into a metal tube to form a "plug."

The seam of the arm can be left open just enough for the plug to be inserted.

If an arm-wire armature is used, the wires can be inserted into the plug tube, then the hand covering fabric may be drawn back over the wrist area (as shown), or it may be inserted into the arm over the wire plug.

THE POSABLE HAND: METHOD II

This method of hand construction can be used with either a machine-sewn glove pattern or a hand sewn, needlesculpted covering. It is possible to create very realistic looking pads of flesh and bony protrusions if a lightweight, stretchy fabric is used with needle-sculpting. Any type of hand construction in cloth can be augmented or additionally sculpted by adding paperclay to the finished, stuffed hand. Heavy-bodied paints will also hide stitches if that is desired.

ABOVE: *The Oldest Elf* by Susanna Oroyan; 24", cloth over wire armature. Pattern model by Susanna Oroyan. Photo by Don Smith.

UPPER RIGHT: *Good Fortune Fairy* by Susanna Oroyan; 24", Ultrasuede over wire armature. Photo by Don Smith.

LOWER RIGHT: *Rings on Her Fingers, Bells on Her Toes* by Susanna Oroyan; 28", cloth. Photo by Don Smith.

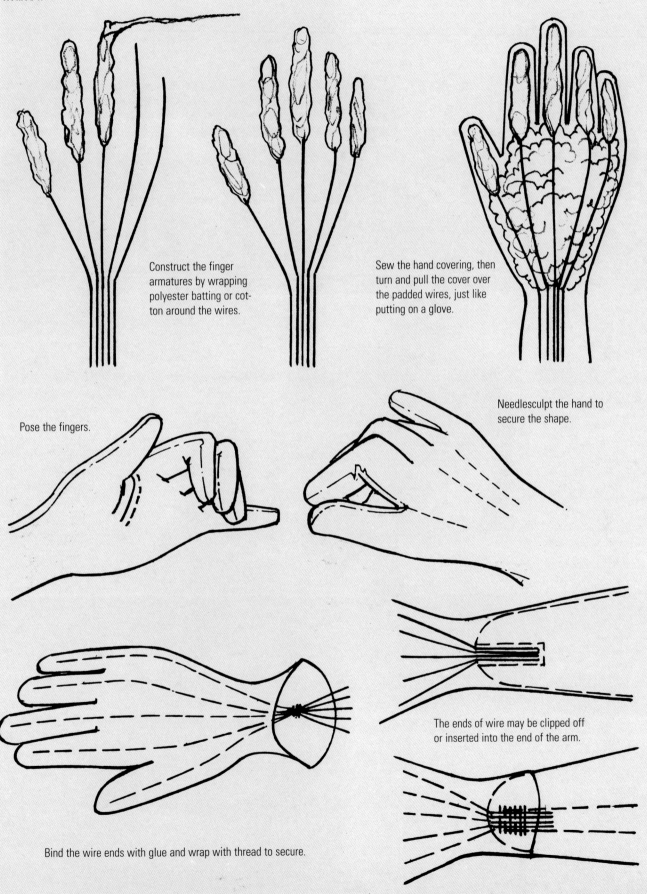

Construct the finger armatures by wrapping polyester batting or cotton around the wires.

Sew the hand covering, then turn and pull the cover over the padded wires, just like putting on a glove.

Pose the fingers.

Needlesculpt the hand to secure the shape.

The ends of wire may be clipped off or inserted into the end of the arm.

Bind the wire ends with glue and wrap with thread to secure.

Feet

For a successful doll design it is very important to have the style of the feet (or shoes) match the type of the hand and style of the head, since these elements are usually the first things the viewer notices. This means that if you choose to make a very realistic head, you are more or less committed to making a fairly realistic set of hands and feet, or shoes. It becomes a matter of design consistency.

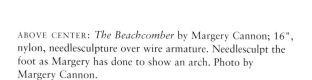

ABOVE CENTER: *The Beachcomber* by Margery Cannon; 16", nylon, needlesculpture over wire armature. Needlesculpt the foot as Margery has done to show an arch. Photo by Margery Cannon.

UPPER RIGHT: *Ondine* by Tomiko Takahashi; 24", cloth over wire armature. Photo by Noboru Takahashi.

LOWER RIGHT: *Red* by Ruth Landis; 18", cloth. Ruth decided that her figure needed accentuated toes, and the flat foot worked well with the other elements of her design, so her foot has an upper and lower piece. Photo by Les Bricker.

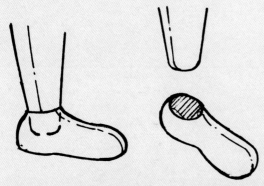

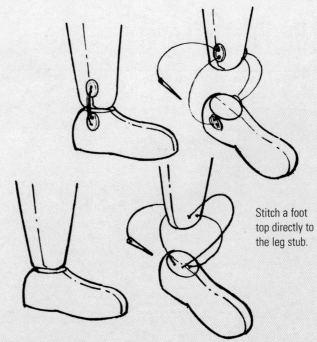

When an arch is desired the foot is constructed as a three-piece pattern with a foot bottom piece or a sole. (Even so, stuffing can still push the foot out of shape. To solve this, we can insert a cardboard inner sole.)

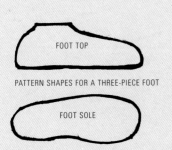

FOOT TOP

PATTERN SHAPES FOR A THREE-PIECE FOOT

FOOT SOLE

NEEDLESCULPTED FOOT TOP

Stitch a foot top directly to the leg stub.

In cloth dollmaking the foot is often made in a different fabric to become the shoe (all in one). The designer looking for a flat foot still has to deal with the "plumping" of the stuffing, and making a decision about where to make the pattern cuts.

A front and side view of a basic leg stitched to show an ankle bend.

PATTERN FOR A BASIC FOOT

PATTERN FOR FOOT WITH DIMENSIONAL TOE

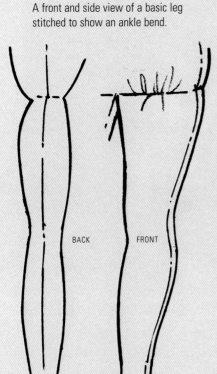

BACK   FRONT

If a shoe is going to be made, the design of the foot needs to be a form or shoe itself. Toes and other bones do not need to be apparent, although we should see the correct shape that the foot would have if they were.

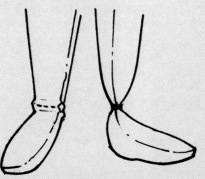

For dimensional toe, bring the foot in together and machine stitch to form toe line.

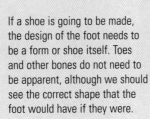

Foot is turned and finished.

The Puzzle Form

Sometimes we have an idea which is conceived from a drawing or as an impression of form or posture. This sort of idea usually does not require movement of the form, although the pose strongly suggests movement. One way to achieve this effect without the use of joints or armature is to create the form from a stacked set of very firmly stuffed parts. To do this you need to sketch your intended shape, then break it down into component parts. Each part becomes a pattern piece for a sewn and stuffed shape.

A Dance in Celebration of Abundance by Karen Wooten; 19", hand-dyed fabric. Pattern for this figure was developed using the modeling techniques taught by Lenore Davis. Photo by Bob Hirsch.

Carmen by Deb Shattil; 18", cloth over armature. Photo by Kate Cameron.

Nefertiti: A Reflection of Beauty by Antonette Cely; 14" seated, cloth. Photo by Don Cely.

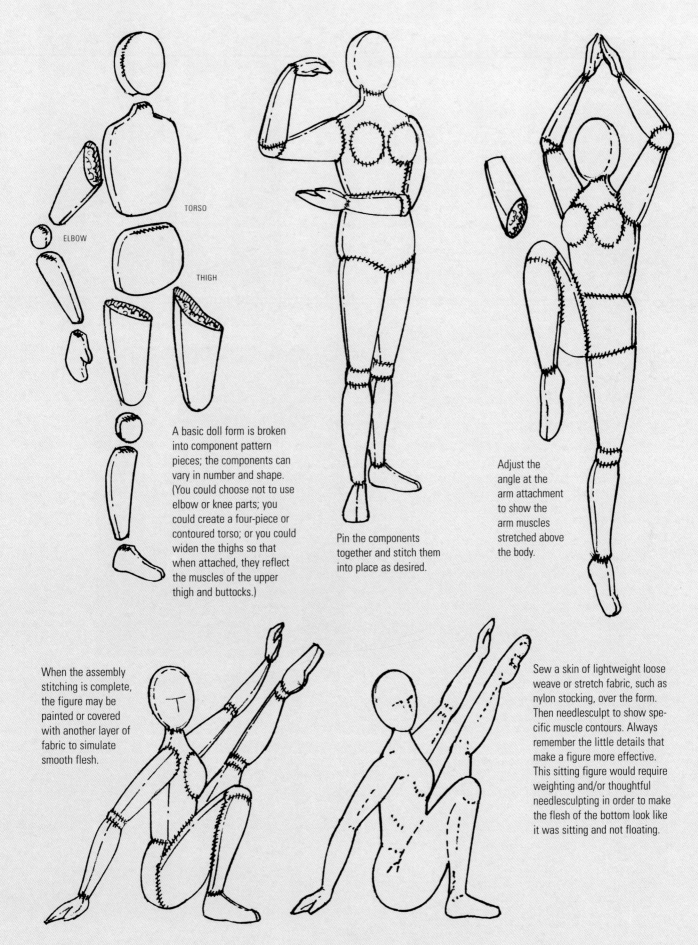

ELBOW

TORSO

THIGH

A basic doll form is broken into component pattern pieces; the components can vary in number and shape. (You could choose not to use elbow or knee parts; you could create a four-piece or contoured torso; or you could widen the thighs so that when attached, they reflect the muscles of the upper thigh and buttocks.)

Pin the components together and stitch them into place as desired.

Adjust the angle at the arm attachment to show the arm muscles stretched above the body.

When the assembly stitching is complete, the figure may be painted or covered with another layer of fabric to simulate smooth flesh.

Sew a skin of lightweight loose weave or stretch fabric, such as nylon stocking, over the form. Then needlesculpt to show specific muscle contours. Always remember the little details that make a figure more effective. This sitting figure would require weighting and/or thoughtful needlesculpting in order to make the flesh of the bottom look like it was sitting and not floating.

Patterns by Draping

We began the section with a discussion of simple two-piece figures, and have gone on to look at a number of ways in which body parts can be constructed so they have three-dimensional character. Before we conclude this section, however, we need to look at the marriage of clay and cloth—the method of developing a whole-body pattern based on an existing solid figure.

The work of the late Lenore Davis started from her exploration of the flat, often monotone form or outline shape that expressed motion. Lenore expanded her figure-making by painting and dying the surface designs. In her later figures she joined the concept of the human form in motion, and the concept of painted details, to figures that were based on completely three-dimensional solids. Lenore's method of creating dimensional figures was adapted from the traditional draping methods used by costumers and fashion designers. Although Lenore's method challenges the cloth dollmaker to undertake clay sculpture, the result will be pattern pieces for sewing that reflect the complex curves of a body in motion and that fit together correctly.

Many doll artists use this same method of draping (sometimes called French Modeling) over a sculpted or stuffed figure to develop tailored costumes that look as if they are moving with the body. When a pattern is developed on paper by design and sketching, there can be quite a bit of trial and error and sewing of experimental pieces until the pattern piece is satisfactory. By using the draping method, however, in just one or two steps the maker is able to create a usable pattern which will reflect the desired human anatomy of the clay model. If you are a costumer, the draping method allows the construction of a basic set of patterns (called a "sloper") that reflect a body. Once this basic pattern is made, it can be redrawn many times, with seam lines reshaped or darts and curves added to make specific fashions.

LEFT: *Dancer Doing a High Kick* by Lenore Davis; 34", painted cloth. Photo courtesy of NIADA Archive.

UPPER RIGHT: *Acrobat on a Pole in Striped Tights* by Lenore Davis; 34", painted cloth. Photo courtesy of NIADA Archive.

CENTER RIGHT: *Acrobat on a Pole in Green Pants* by Lenore Davis; 34", painted cloth. Photo courtesy of NIADA Archive.

LOWER RIGHT: *Acrobat on a Pole in Blue Pants* by Lenore Davis; 34", painted cloth. Photo courtesy of NIADA Archive.

Fitting a fabric body pattern as Lenore Davis might have done. This method allows a complex pattern to be accurately developed. The pattern pieces created by draping are trimmed and given a uniform seam allowance. The heavy lines become the finished seam lines.

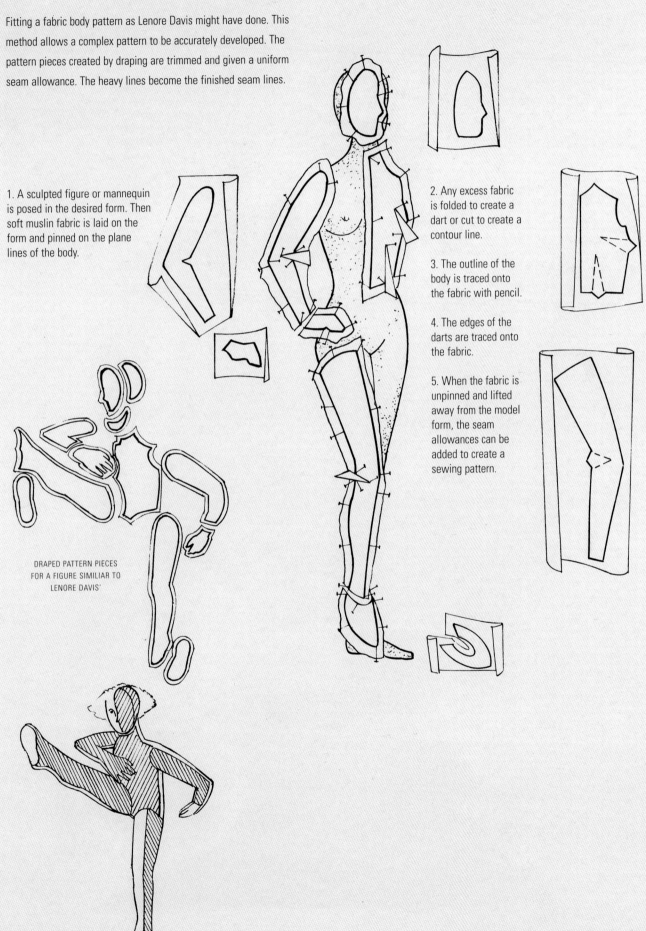

1. A sculpted figure or mannequin is posed in the desired form. Then soft muslin fabric is laid on the form and pinned on the plane lines of the body.

2. Any excess fabric is folded to create a dart or cut to create a contour line.

3. The outline of the body is traced onto the fabric with pencil.

4. The edges of the darts are traced onto the fabric.

5. When the fabric is unpinned and lifted away from the model form, the seam allowances can be added to create a sewing pattern.

DRAPED PATTERN PIECES
FOR A FIGURE SIMILIAR TO
LENORE DAVIS'

Celtic Goddess of the Moon by Lawan Angelique; 21", needlesculpted stockinette (detail below). Photo by Christina Florkowski.

UPPER LEFT: *Owl Deva* by Akira Blount; 24", leather and cloth, jointed body. Photo by David Luttrel.

UPPER RIGHT: *The Reader* by Barbara Buysse; 12", oil paint on linen. Photo by Douglas Neal.

LOWER RIGHT: *Spirit of Change* by Kath Lathers; 20", cloth. Photo by Pete Draugalis.

UPPER LEFT: *Astar* by Lisa L. Lichtenfels; 38", nylon stocking over wire armature. Photo by Lisa L. Lichtenfels.

UPPER RIGHT: *The Protective Spirit* by Gretchen Lima; 24", sculpted face and hand, cloth body, leather shield. Photo by Bill Lemke.

LOWER LEFT: *Nizhoni* by Helen Pringle; 21", cotton, oil painted. Photo by Don Smith.

UPPER LEFT: *Famous Face-Mona Lisa* by Pamela Hastings; 9", laminated paper applied to fabric. Photo by David Egan.

LOWER LEFT: *Rockettes* by Ellen Rixford; 4½ feet, mechanical, nylon, and other fabrics over hard foam and wood. Photo by Ellen Rixford.

RIGHT: *Lucia* by Shelley Thornton; 28", stuffed cotton knit, wood ball joints, needlesculpted and embroidered face. Photo by Roger Bruhn.

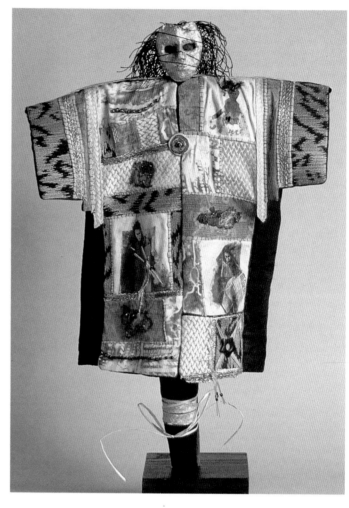

UPPER LEFT: *Going Fishing* by Hedy Katin; 18", cloth. Photo by Les Bricker.

UPPER RIGHT: *The Mask* by Carol Stygles; 28", paperclay, silk, found materials. Photo by Les Bricker.

LOWER RIGHT: *Mermaid* by Dawn Kinsey; 14", needlesculpted silk. Photo by Dawn Kinsey.

UPPER LEFT: *Very Soon and in Pleasant Company* by Zhenne Wood, Dollmaker; 24", one-of-a-kind cloth doll, painted silk face, body of antique kimono, pincushion babies, bamboo ornaments, and Chinese cookie fortune, 1990. Photo by David Bigelow.

UPPER RIGHT: *Miranda Carmen* by Julie McCullough; 28", Lycra over needlesculpture. Photo by John Nollendorfs.

LOWER LEFT: *Reba* by Beverly Dodge Radefeld; 15", cloth, needlesculpted. Photo by Les Bricker.

UPPER LEFT: *The Midnight Mermaid* by Julie McCullough; 24", cloth, painted. Photo by Les Bricker.

UPPER RIGHT: *Botticelli Maidens* by Jacqueline Casey; 18", cloth. Photo by Jacqueline Casey.

LOWER LEFT: *Angel Alighting* by Barbara Chapman; 20", cloth, bead embellishments. Photo by Les Bricker.

UPPER LEFT: *Feeding the Birds* by Margery Cannon; 16", nylon needle-sculpture over wire armature. Photo by Margery Cannon.

UPPER RIGHT: *The Herbalist* by Doree Pitkin; 24", cloth. Photo by Doree Pitkin.

LOWER RIGHT: *Praying for Healing* by Kareena Bouse; 20", silk over sculpted head. Photo by Bob Hirsch.

BODY JOINTS
Decorative Joints

Simple cloth joints—stitched, tied, ball, or slipped bead types—are not truly working joints. Although they accentuate a movement, or allow a figure to sit more easily, they are primarily for design interest. When solving a joint problem, we have to consider the actual motion of each individual joint: hips are ball and socket, a knee is a hinge, and none of the human joints revolve in a full circle. When you think about it, there are probably several complex ways joints can be contoured and assembled in cloth. However, it is at this point when we are tempted to say, "what for?"; meaning, "why do all that work for just a doll?" The answer is likened to the idea of climbing a mountain: Because I had the idea and it might look good for this figure concept.

Hawk Woman by Julie McCullough;
34", velour, button joints.
Photo by John Nollendorfs.

Tahlia by Bonnie Hoover; 17", button joints.
Photo by Sandra Hoover.

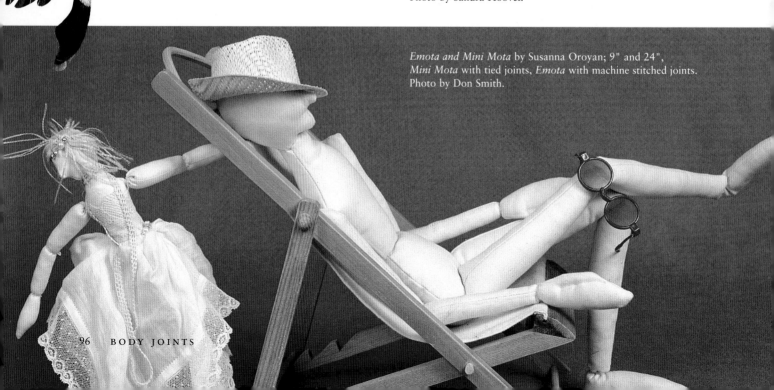

Emota and Mini Mota by Susanna Oroyan; 9" and 24",
Mini Mota with tied joints, *Emota* with machine stitched joints.
Photo by Don Smith.

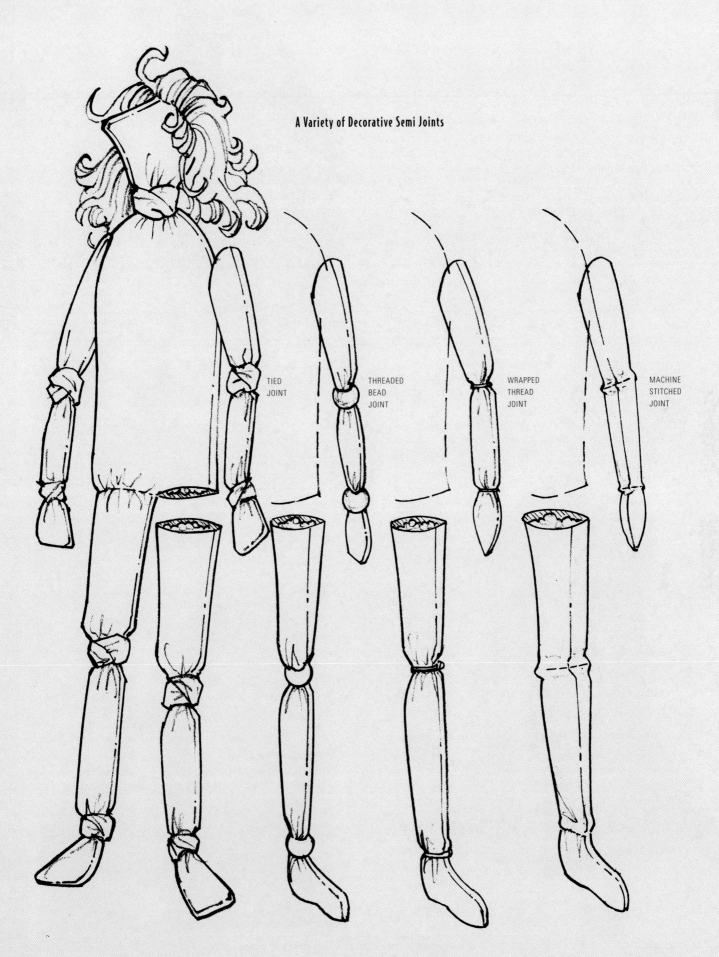

A Variety of Decorative Semi Joints

TIED
JOINT

THREADED
BEAD
JOINT

WRAPPED
THREAD
JOINT

MACHINE
STITCHED
JOINT

Joint Options

In order to achieve a well-designed doll, all the elements that you combine and all the choices that you make will require good reasons. When you choose to use one of the decorative, non-functioning joints, it is probably because you want to underline or delineate the idea that humans have parts (bones) that can move. Using a decorative bead or a metallic thread to make this delineation also provides more scope for working with texture and color. However, when you choose to include a functioning joint in your design, your reason needs to be a bit more specific because a functioning joint system implies a player. What is it that you want the player to be able to do? Do you want to limit or direct the play?

As shown in the photographs, doll designer Maggie Iacono wants her player to be able to play with the doll as they would a toy. Her dolls, therefore, incorporate the traditional ball and socket joint used in composition dollmaking. Making this type of a joint in fabric requires complex interior stringing as well as solving problems of achieving the necessary tension with soft parts. At the other extreme, the designer can elect to make very simple body connections, as in the marionette and non-jointed examples. With these the player can manipulate the figure in continuous motion (as in a working marionette) or position it to show a wide range of human action or emotion. There are many choices. Think about which choice will be the right one for your idea.

Body by Maggie Iacono; 17", note the joint construction. Photo by Maggie Iacono.

Mary Quite Contrary by Maggie Iacono; 17", felt, dress embellished with stencil, ribbon embroidery, and felt appliqué. Photo by Maggie Iacono.

Boy with a Velveteen Rabbit and Rebecca by Maggie Iacono; 17", pressed felt, wood ball and socket joints. Photo by Maggie Iacono.

Marionette Joint   The most simple articulated joint in cloth is similar to a marionette joint. Movement is achieved by breaking the limbs of arms and legs entirely, and then stitching together the joints.

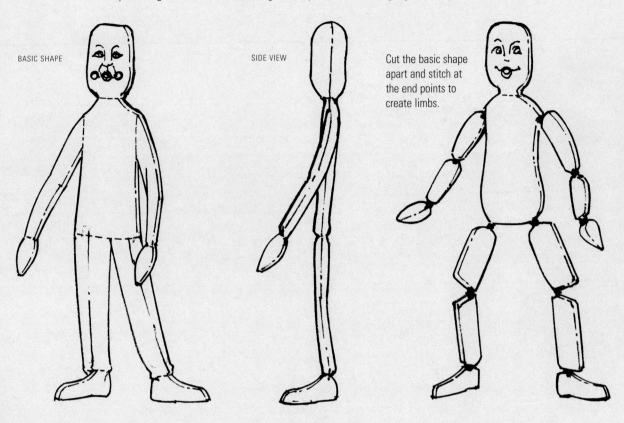

BASIC SHAPE

SIDE VIEW

Cut the basic shape apart and stitch at the end points to create limbs.

The Non-Joint   Movement can be suggested when the hands and feet are connected by gathering and sewing them to costume parts. The costume is constructed to hold together the hands and feet.

The Bead Joint

Bead joints are primarily decorative and will not hold a pose. But sooner or later in our search to make doll figures simulate a real human—to sit up, or stand up and behave—we find we need to make a joint that will hold a pose. Although the bead joint is primarily for decorative interest, it can create a posable, non-floppy bend if the beads are wired. Here we can have the advantage of an interior wire armature to hold a pose and, using a bead, a visible exterior joint area.

Brother and Sister by Susanna Oroyan; 12", bead joints, painted cloth. Photo by Don Smith.

Arthritis Doll by Virginia Robertson; 12", bead joints. Photo by Virginia Robertson.

Scrap doll by Virginia Robertson; 12", bead joints. Photo by Virginia Robertson.

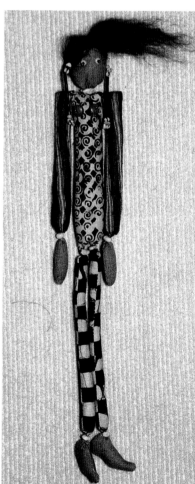

Reflections by Elaine Anne Spence; 12", stitched joints with handmade button detail. Photo by Don Smith.

The Wired Bead Joint

The process is rather like stringing beads. Start with the wire armature and a partially stuffed limb.

Set the wire armature into a nest of stuffing at the end of the limb.

Stuff the limb to the joint, then slip a bead down the wire to the joint area.

Stuff the limb next to the joint area.

Secure the bead in place by gathering stitches at its top and bottom.

DETAIL OF WIRE

Attach limb to body.

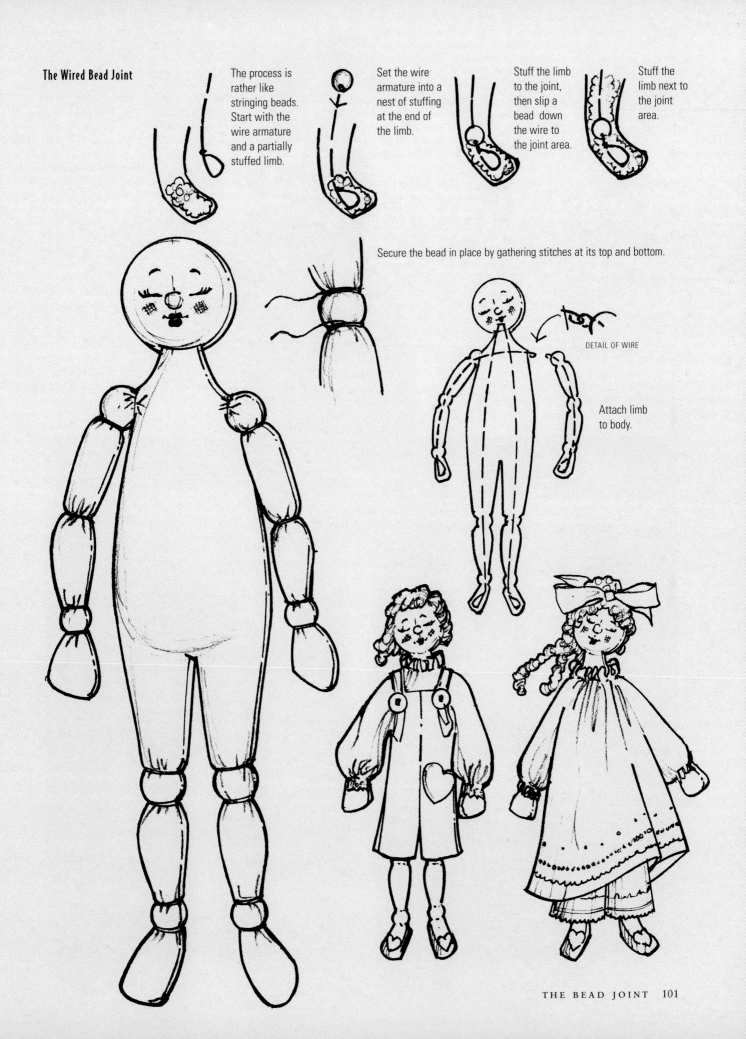

The Stitched Bead Joint

Shelly Thornton achieved her solution to the problem of creating a directed motion by modifying the stitched bead joint. This joint is actually quite human-like in that it combines the ball and socket contruction of the actual joint with the expansion and contraction of the tendons. Using the thread to simulate tendons also keeps the limb from turning from side to side in non-human motion. Although the visual appearance is quite different, note that the button and gusset joints on the following pages also function as tendons that limit side-to-side limb motion.

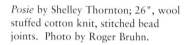

Asha and the Moon Ball by Shelley Thornton; 25", cotton knit. Photo by Don Smith.

Amelia Undressed by Shelley Thornton; 24", cotton knit, stitched bead joints, body joints designed. Photo by Ron Brown.

Posie by Shelley Thornton; 26", wool stuffed cotton knit, stitched bead joints. Photo by Roger Bruhn.

The Stitched Bead Joint   The stitched bead joint can reflect true joints in that the bead is placed between the two soft parts of the limb so that the joint can move freely and hold a position. An additional advantage of a joint of this type is that its movement is limited by the direction of the stringing pattern so that the limb can only move in directions that reflect human motion.

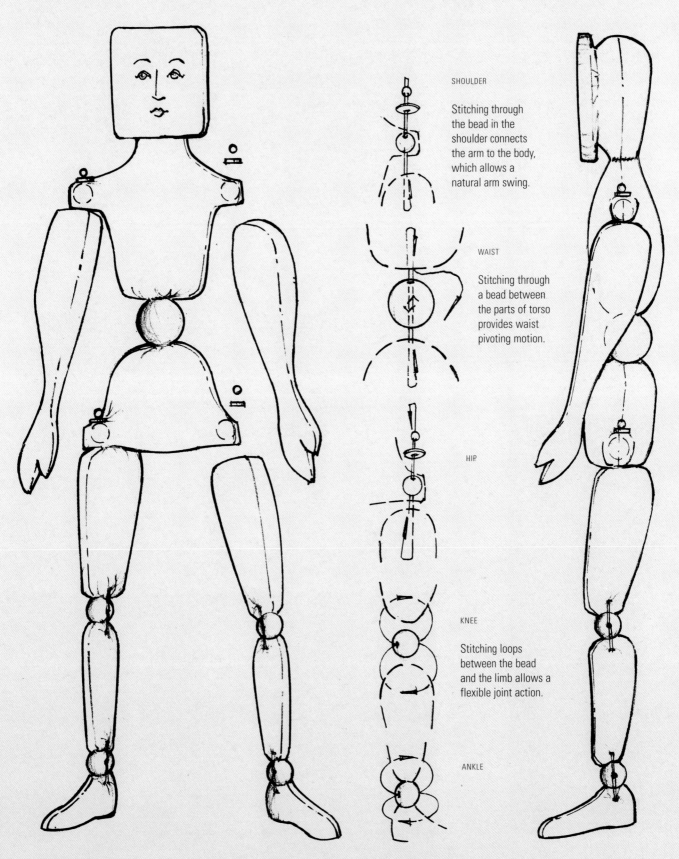

SHOULDER

Stitching through the bead in the shoulder connects the arm to the body, which allows a natural arm swing.

WAIST

Stitching through a bead between the parts of torso provides waist pivoting motion.

HIP

KNEE

Stitching loops between the bead and the limb allows a flexible joint action.

ANKLE

The Button Joint

Traditionally, motion in figures has often been achieved by stringing the limbs together by sewing through the body. Although this seems like an easy solution, the element of physics enters in: thread or string stitched through fabric, once pulled and secured to hold the pieces against the body, puts tension on the fabric of the limbs. Sooner, and certainly later, tension wears a hole through the fabric, and the thread will break after repeated movement. The solution that spreads out the forces of the thread tension and that provides a base to pull against is the old-fashioned, plain, button.

To closely match actual human movement, a dollmaker could use a combination of joints. Adding an interior wire armature would imitate the element of tendon and muscle movement so that the figure could be bent and held in place in defiance of gravity. With any of the methods shown, whether by adding beads, buttons, or stringing joints, a jointed figure could then be covered by a smooth "skin" made from fabric or leather. Imagine what such a figure might look like if covered with an elasticized fabric such as Lycra...almost real!

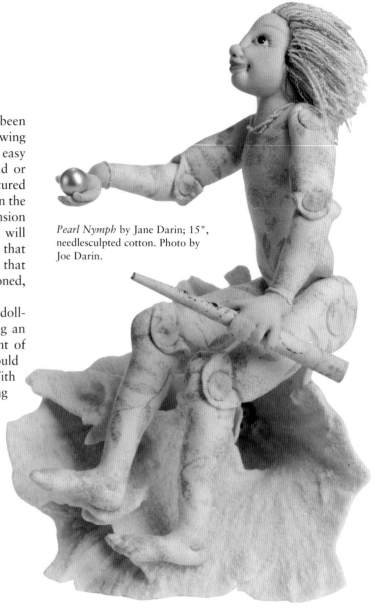

Pearl Nymph by Jane Darin; 15", needlesculpted cotton. Photo by Joe Darin.

Jester by Akira Blount; 26", needlesculpted, button joints. Photo by David Luttrel.

Study Model by Susanna Oroyan; 24", felt, painted face. Photo by Don Smith.

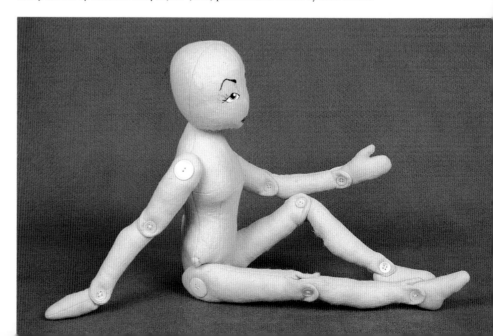

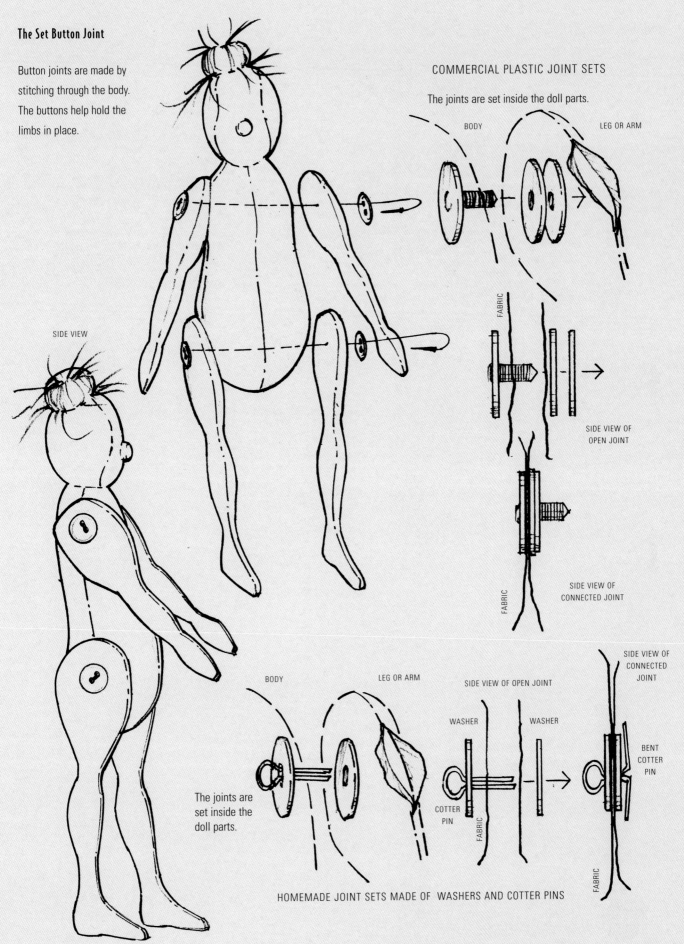

The Set Button Joint

Button joints are made by stitching through the body. The buttons help hold the limbs in place.

SIDE VIEW

COMMERCIAL PLASTIC JOINT SETS

The joints are set inside the doll parts.

BODY

LEG OR ARM

FABRIC

SIDE VIEW OF
OPEN JOINT

FABRIC

SIDE VIEW OF
CONNECTED JOINT

The joints are set inside the doll parts.

BODY

LEG OR ARM

SIDE VIEW OF OPEN JOINT

SIDE VIEW OF
CONNECTED
JOINT

WASHER

WASHER

BENT
COTTER
PIN

COTTER
PIN

FABRIC

FABRIC

HOMEMADE JOINT SETS MADE OF WASHERS AND COTTER PINS

The Tabbed Button Joint

Taken one step further, the exterior buttons can become part of a joint hidden within the body. In most doll design this kind of joint is only used at the shoulder and hip. However, if it can go on the outside, it can go inside the body, too. It becomes a design challenge for dollmakers to find or make joints small enough to work for the dolls they are creating.

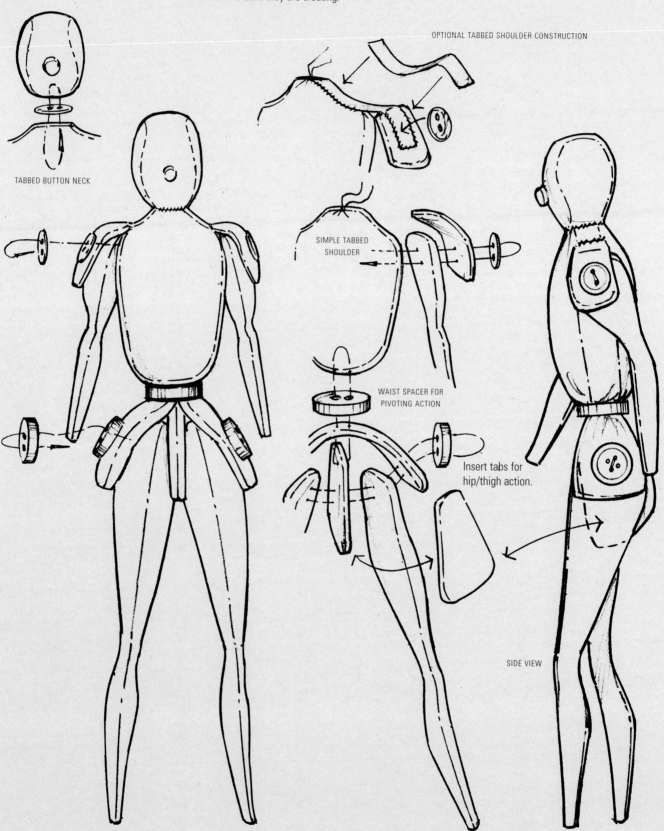

OPTIONAL TABBED SHOULDER CONSTRUCTION

TABBED BUTTON NECK

SIMPLE TABBED SHOULDER

WAIST SPACER FOR PIVOTING ACTION

Insert tabs for hip/thigh action.

SIDE VIEW

The Gusseted Button Joint

Some dollmakers enjoy the challenge of making a figure as real as possible. The ultimate jointing for a figure in cloth would be one which combines either the ball and socket or strung joint and the mortise and tenon joint, such as the gusseted button joint.

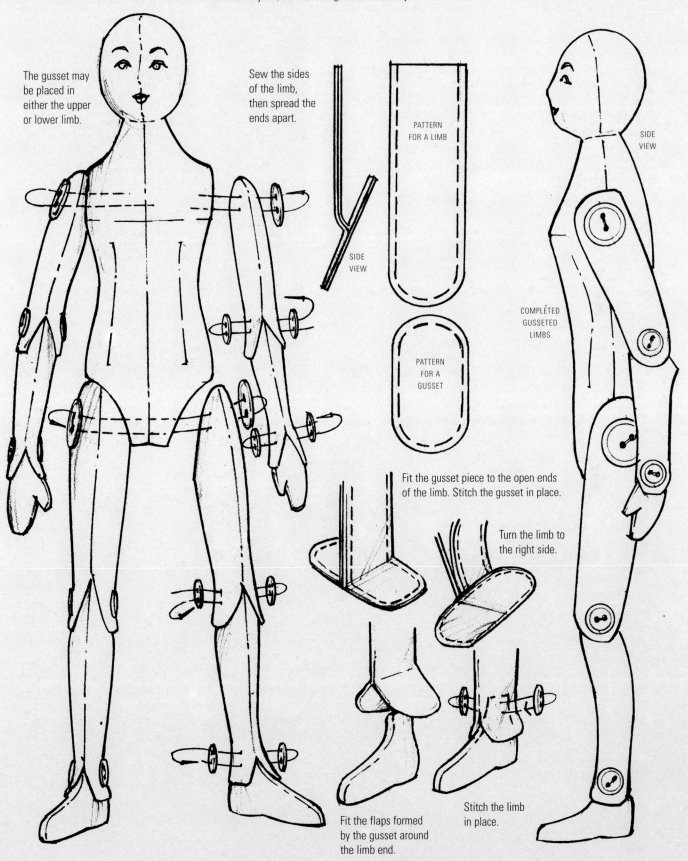

The gusset may be placed in either the upper or lower limb.

Sew the sides of the limb, then spread the ends apart.

SIDE VIEW

PATTERN FOR A LIMB

PATTERN FOR A GUSSET

SIDE VIEW

COMPLETED GUSSETED LIMBS

Fit the gusset piece to the open ends of the limb. Stitch the gusset in place.

Turn the limb to the right side.

Fit the flaps formed by the gusset around the limb end.

Stitch the limb in place.

ASSEMBLIES
Working the Wire

Next to cloth, wire is probably the most important material in dollmaking. I always find it amazing when I hear an otherwise experienced dollmaker describe a problem that could have been easily solved by using wire. Everyone, it seems, should know about the use of wire in body making because wire has been traditionally and universally used for centuries. When I first started making dolls in the 1960s, there were less than a half dozen books on dollmaking; yet every one of them showed some form of wire armature construction. Unfortunately, many of the books and publications which described the various wire applications have had short shelf-lives or are very difficult to find. Perhaps some dollmakers do not want to attempt wire armatures because the process looks complicated and difficult. Although it is awkward to deal with floppy loops and ends that whip in the initial stages, the results are well worth the effort of mastering the technique.

What kind of wire should you use? Many kinds. And have a selection on hand. The types of wire are denoted by gauge. The smaller the number (or gauge), the thicker the wire. For doll bodies in the 10" to 24" range, 16 gauge galvanized (non-rusting) wire will be strong enough to support a head of porcelain or polymer clay. If economy is a factor, electrical fencing wire (17 gauge) comes in large rolls. Aluminum, copper, and bronze-colored craft wire can be found in jewelry sections of craft shops in the 18 to 30 gauge. Fine wire is handy for a number of purposes, but 20 gauge is best for figures from 3" to 10" tall. Copper wire is tempting, but often too soft for making a well-engineered support. Generally, aluminum wire is best. Aluminum sculpture wire is very flexible, very strong, and relatively inexpensive. It comes in widths up to ¼" thick. Also, electrical cable (interior wall type) and the ordinary coat hanger both have their uses in dollmaking.

Christmas Memories by Margery Cannon; 24", cloth, wire armature. Photo by Margery Cannon.

Festival Later by Tomiko Takahashi; 12", cloth. Photo by Noburo Takahashi.

Adam and Eve by Akiko Anzai; 18" cloth, wire armature. Photo by Les Bricker.

If your chosen pose is a position where a human would have to use extra muscle power against gravity to maintain it, you might have to add weight to your figure. Sew a small bag, fill it with lead or copper weights, and stitch or wire it into the lower torso. If your figure will have an exceptionally heavy torso or head, you might retrace the steps for creating the back and legs, thus doubling the wires.

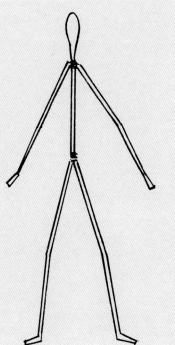

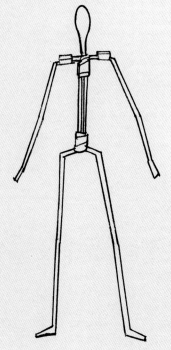

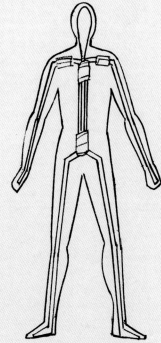

Always keep the wires parallel.

Do not twist the wires except to tuck in the ends. Remember, twisted wires make springs and you probably want strength rather than bounce.

Apply tape as you work to keep the wires parallel and more manageable. Always create your figure with width at the shoulder and hip. The shoulder should always be wide enough to allow the arm to hang outside the hip.

When you have finished your armature, stand it up and bend it until it balances by itself. A well-made figure should stand by itself.

You can accentuate a male, female, or generic body by wrapping the wire, as shown. Cardboard templates or body shapes can also be used to fill out the base form outline of the finished figure.

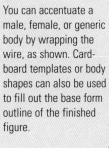

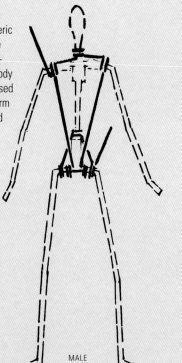

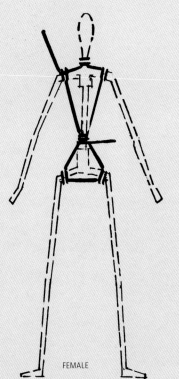

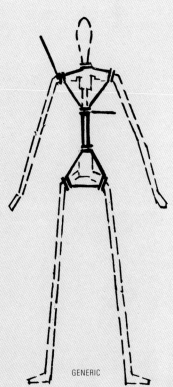

MALE

FEMALE

GENERIC

The Wire Armature

Before constructing a wire armature it is best to have an idea of how large the finished figure will be. If you have already made a head, here is the formula for ascertaining adult height in a doll: Multiply the height of the head by eight. For example, if the doll's head measures 2½" from chin to top of head, the total height of the body should be 20" (8 x 2.5 = 20). True human scale is 7.5 heads equal the body height; however, as dolls are commonly viewed by looking down on them, which foreshortens the figure, we usually put more length in the leg. A child's proportions, depending on age, will be between 4 and 7 heads. Most artist anatomy reference books give proportions for typical ages.

Once you have determined the height of the figure, sketch the shape you want, keeping fairly true to correct human anatomical proportions. Abstract or purposely exaggerated figures are more successful if they are exaggerations of the basic human shape. But always make sure that any abstracted or exaggerated form is balanced in design. For example, if you make the legs longer, then the arms should also be longer. Remember, any time you vary from the norm you must pay special attention to creating a harmonious, visual pattern or overall design. It is fine to jolt the viewer's expectation, but it won't work unless you provide the person with an understandable system.

Moth Nymph by Dawn Kinsey; 8", silk, needlesculpture. Photo by Chester Majak.

Today I Shall Forgo the Hoop by Maggie Mayer; 21", cloth, needlesculpture. Photo by Maggie Mayer.

The illustration is drawn from a 4" figure constructed of 20 gauge copper wire that was intended for dollhouse use.

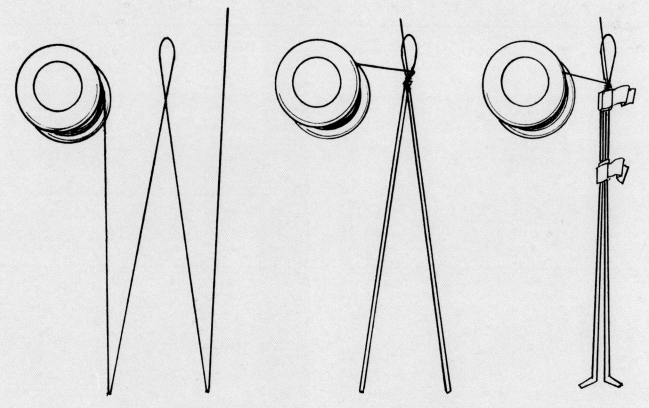

1. Make a "W" shape. The loop will support a head.

2. Twist the ends together at the neck.

3. Tape the torso below the neck and above the hip.

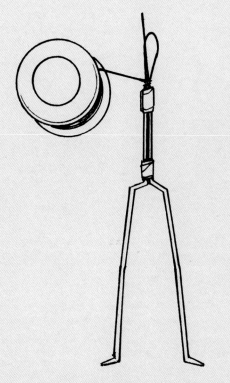

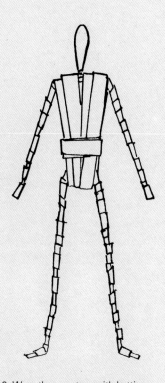

4. Bend to form the hips.

5. Bend wire to form arms, and tape at the shoulders.

6. Wrap the armature with batting.

Inserting the Wire

When a wire armature is inserted into a cloth body, the resulting doll moves toward becoming a purely esthetic form. The maker has total control over the look of the piece. The maker can experiment with poses and arrange the body and limbs to express a particular action or motion...and have the satisfaction of knowing they will stay that way.

Leap Frogs by Dawn Kinsey; 10", silk needlesculpture, paperclay. Photo by Dawn Kinsey.

The Gift by Susanna Oroyan; 15", cloth, wire armature. Photo by Don Smith.

This series of photos by Molly Cokeley show how to cover a figure that has an inserted wire armature. Notice how nicely a balancing posture is achieved with the wire.

1. The figure shown has an inserted armature.

2. When the figure is positioned as desired, it is covered with pieces of nylon stocking.

3. Padding under the stocking creates a form which accentuates the pose.

4. The finished figure. Even though you may not see the actual tummy and bottom shapes, the fact that they are there makes the costume drape most effectively.

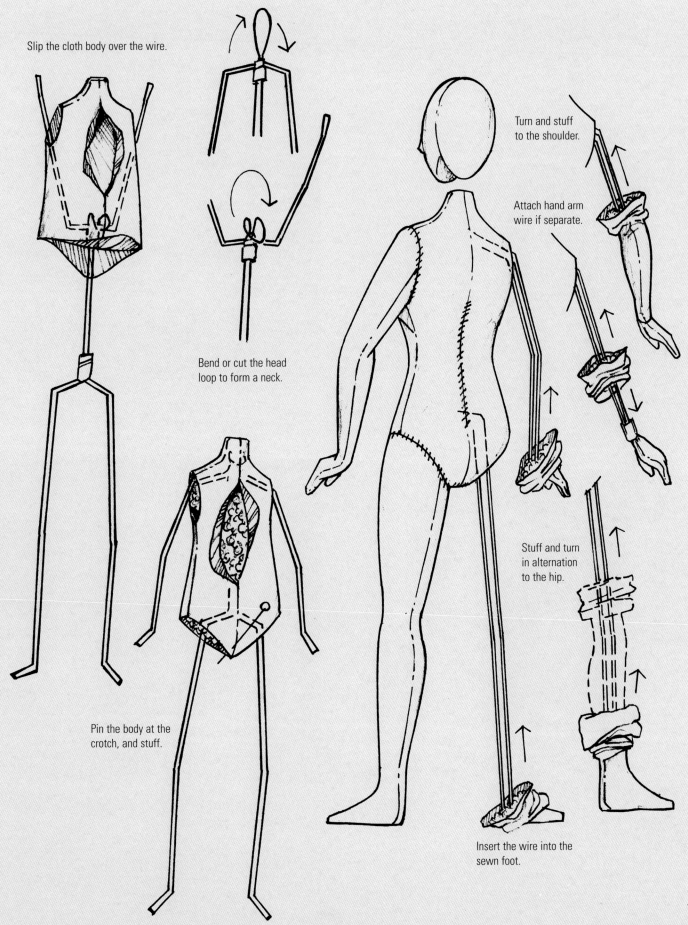

Slip the cloth body over the wire.

Bend or cut the head loop to form a neck.

Turn and stuff to the shoulder.

Attach hand arm wire if separate.

Stuff and turn in alternation to the hip.

Pin the body at the crotch, and stuff.

Insert the wire into the sewn foot.

Covering the Wire

French Maid by Terry Irick; 48", velour, wire armature. Photo by Ute Compton.

There are any number of ways a creative dollmaker can use the wire armature for creating a finished piece. One method is to wrap strips of quilt batting, cloth, string, or yarn around the wired form to pad out the figure. Or, the unpadded framework can be inserted into sewn cloth body parts and then stuffed. If sculpted parts have been made previously, the armature can be shortened to the length necessary to attach hands/arms or legs/feet. Wood or previously sculpted clay parts can be drilled for the insertion of wire. The bare wire armature, wrapped with masking tape, can be used as a base for sculpting with paperclay products. Or, if you want to build a needlesculpted figure from the muscles outward, you can construct your armature with space between the arm and leg wires so that fabric padding can be stitched on and between the wires. If you choose to cover the wire, any of these methods will produce a delightful human-like figure.

A Dull Day by Keiko Asami; 18", cloth, wire armature. Photo by Teruo Shimizu.

Children on a Bicycle by Tomiko Takahashi; 14", cloth, wire armature. Photo by Noboru Takahashi.

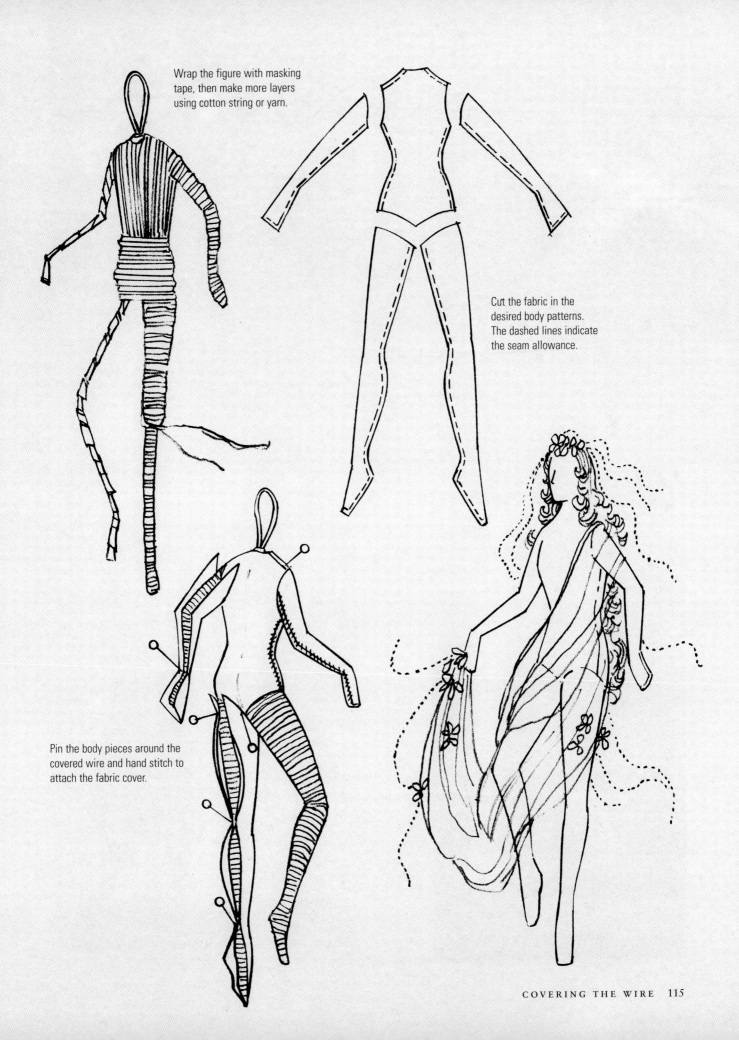

Wrap the figure with masking tape, then make more layers using cotton string or yarn.

Cut the fabric in the desired body patterns. The dashed lines indicate the seam allowance.

Pin the body pieces around the covered wire and hand stitch to attach the fabric cover.

Fixed Figures

Any dollmaker who specializes in showing off fabric surfaces, or creating period or character costuming, can use the fixed wire figure construction method to advantage. The coat hanger wire and cloth armature allows the maker to create a posable, sculptural upper body without having to go into great structural detail below the waist (where the anatomy will not be seen or where it is not necessary to create form). With this method, the figures are usually covered or draped in a costume that reaches the ground or, if shorter, only the tips of the shoes or feet show. The method is also used for figures that bend or sway in positions that are difficult to achieve balance. Although a simplified body form is illustrated, the maker has the option of using any type of head, bust, and hand construction one might need or prefer to complete the form.

Sulkey Challenge '95 by Susanna Oroyan; 6", cloth, wire armature. Photo by Susanna Oroyan.

Titania and Oberon by Maggie Mayer; 18", cloth, needlesculpted. Photo by Maggie Mayer.

Emily by Susanna Oroyan; 16", cloth, wire armature. Photo by Susanna Oroyan.

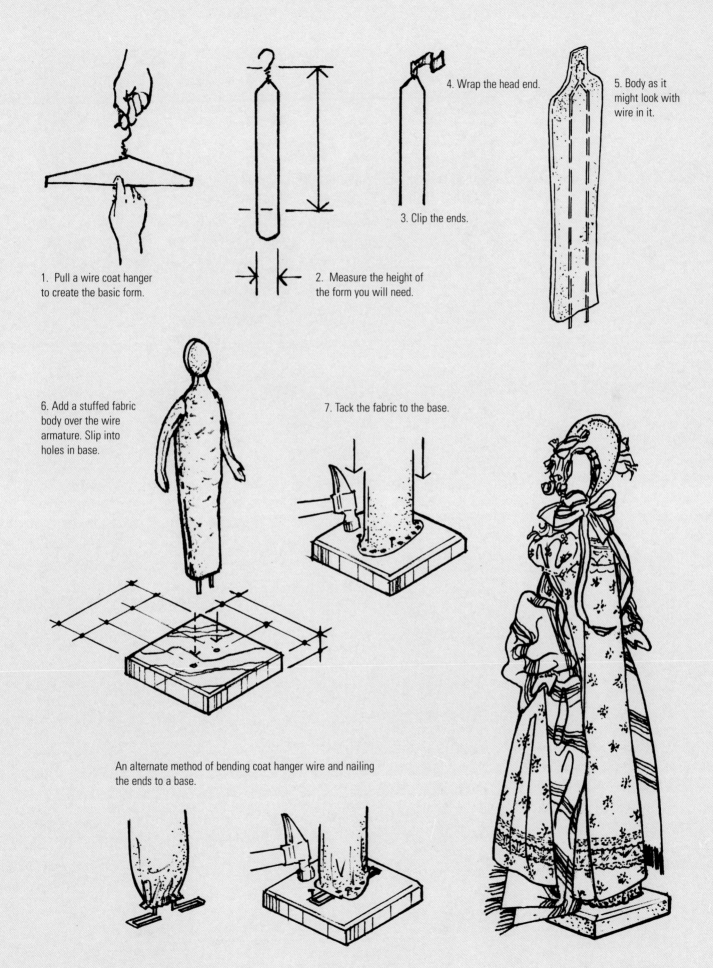

1. Pull a wire coat hanger to create the basic form.

2. Measure the height of the form you will need.

3. Clip the ends.

4. Wrap the head end.

5. Body as it might look with wire in it.

6. Add a stuffed fabric body over the wire armature. Slip into holes in base.

7. Tack the fabric to the base.

An alternate method of bending coat hanger wire and nailing the ends to a base.

UPPER LEFT: *The Fabric Clown* by Jane Davies; 30", fabric-covered mask. Photo by Les Bricker.

UPPER RIGHT: *Clown "Hallo!"* by Akiko Sasaki; 17", cloth. Photo by Akiko Sasaki.

LOWER LEFT: *Women of Color* by Sandra Feingold; 13," painted muslin. Photo by Bob Hirsch.

UPPER LEFT: *Woman of Light* by Marcella Welch; 18", cloth over resin. Photo by Jerry Anthony Studios.

UPPER RIGHT: *Stargaze Rainbow* by Patti Medaris Culea; 20", hand-dyed silk charmeuse, wire armature. Photo by Bob Hirsch.

LOWER LEFT: *Someone to Lean On* by Patricia Coleman-Cobb; 21", cloth. Photo by Les Bricker.

UPPER LEFT: *Birthday Girl* by Caty Carlin; 22", hand-painted cotton. Photo by Don Smith.

LOWER LEFT: *Minstral* by Nancy J. Laverick; 11", Ultrasuede over wire armature. Photo by Nancy J. Laverick.

LOWER RIGHT: *Friends* by Virginia Robertson; 12", cloth. Photo by Virginia Robertson.

UPPER LEFT: *Got a Kettle on My Head Blues* by elinor peace bailey; 24", cloth. Photo by Isaac A.R. Bailey.

LOWER LEFT: *Clairvoyant* by Sara Austin; 26", cloth. Photo by Les Bricker.

LOWER RIGHT: *Madam Chairperson* by elinor peace bailey; 24", cloth. Photo by Les Bricker.

TOP: *Lion Man, Laughing Jamaican, Jumpsuit Girl and Red Monkey Man Have a Conversation* by Andra Dunn; 30", cloth with papier mâché masks. Photo by Andra Dunn.

LOWER LEFT: *Johann and Christian* by Frances Petefish; 9" and 6", needlesculpted cotton. Photo by Bob Hirsch.

LOWER RIGHT: *Heavens, It's High Tea* by Ann Woodman; 14", cloth. Photo by Ann Woodman.

UPPER LEFT: *Fleurette* by Bonnie Stewart; 20", cotton head painted and glazed. Photo by Bob Hirsch.

UPPER RIGHT: *Rosie and Her Red Hat* by Becky Craver; 14 ½", needlesculpted Lycra. Photo by Becky Craver.

LOWER LEFT: *Valentine* by Barbara Willis; 23", jointed cloth. Photo by Photomaster.

LOWER RIGHT: *Mabel* by Tracy Page Stillwell; 12", pieced cotton, hand-painted. Photo by Beth Ludwig.

UPPER LEFT: *Champagne Dreams* by Antonette Cely; 13" seated, cloth. Photo by Don Cely.

LOWER LEFT: *Girl with Jumping Rope* by Junko Liesfeld; 8", cloth. Photo by Don Smith.

LOWER RIGHT: *Gift of the Druid Queen* by Karen Wooten; 16", wrapped wire armature, handpainted doe skin. Photo by Bob Hirsch.

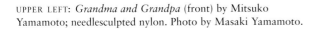

UPPER LEFT: *Grandma and Grandpa* (front) by Mitsuko Yamamoto; needlesculpted nylon. Photo by Masaki Yamamoto.

LOWER LEFT: *Grandma and Grandpa* (back) by Mitsuko Yamamoto; needlesculpted nylon. Photo by Masaki Yamamoto.

UPPER RIGHT: *Me and My Shadow* by Marla Florio; 14" and 15", cloth. Photo by Les Bricker.

LOWER RIGHT: *Celeste* by Caterine Fulton; 17", soft-sculpted cotton. Photo by Bob Hirsch.

UPPER LEFT: *Guardian Angel* by Miriam Gourley; 12", cloth, built-up paperclay face. Photo by Darrel Jensen.

UPPER RIGHT: *Courting the Flame* by Maggie Mayer; 21", painted cloth. Photo by Maggie Mayer.

LOWER LEFT: *Enchanted April* by Christine Shively; 28", painted and embroidered cloth. Photo by Azad.

LOWER RIGHT: *Shaunté* by Carla Thompson; 18", painted head, cloth. Photo by Carla Thompson.

UPPER LEFT: *The Doll Judge* by Bonnie Boots; 18", needlesculpted nylon stocking over padded fleece. Photo by Bonnie Boots.

UPPER RIGHT: *Magical Matilda* by Susan Hale; 22", painted canvas. Photo by Susan Hale.

LOWER LEFT: *Tilly Willow Dolls* by Catherine Fulton; 17", cotton soft sculpture. Photo by Bob Hirsch.

As you look through this book, you can see that doll-making consists of about a dozen primary techniques that are infinitely varied by the artist's individuality, interest, material choices, and construction preferences.

Most dollmakers start with an idea, which is a picture or visualization of the finished figure. Usually, that visualization will be closely connected with a construction technique—modeled clay or needlesculpted cloth, joint mechanics, pattern outline, or color, texture, and pattern. A very good example of specific idea visualization was reported by Althea Church. When she was working on her dolls while traveling on a train, she wished she had little drawers built into her body so she could carry along her dollmaking supplies. Althea challenged herself to create a doll that had drawers, and the result was her *Traveling Dollmaker*.

No matter how you see your idea, you will have to build the form. In Althea's case, she worked with a variation of the basic cloth doll. In order to make operable drawers, she had to make a frame to hold them, insert it into the body, then build drawers to fit the frame. Her challenge was in making the actual mechanics within the form.

When the form is done, we face the initial challenge: How to complete the doll as you imagined it—or near to it. Sometimes, we change in midstream and get really interesting surprises. Even Althea had to make clothes, hair, and the right accessories within the design framework for the type of doll she chose. Completing the piece for most of us is the part that is the most fun. Here we can delineate the character with clothing, embellishments, and accessories.

Usually, we have some notion about how to do it or what we will use, but the following few general suggestions are for your consideration.

COSTUMING

Many dollmakers have no difficulty when sewing and stuffing a body, or when creating a head. But when it comes to costuming, some get spooked. Will it help if I say there are no rules? Will it help if I say you can do anything you like as long as it works for you?

Many beginners think in terms of costuming a doll as they would a real human: clothes that look real or that can be changed. A doll that is to be played with really must have removable clothing. But a doll that is to be looked at does not. In either case, the maker really becomes a fashion designer.

Even if you begin with an idea of what your doll will look like in clothes, you are always well-advised to have at least one or two books in your library which show photographs and drawings of costume throughout history. Try to make good use of your public library and doll book distributor's catalogs to find specific how-to books for pattern and accessory construction. In addition to the reference material, your knowledge of home sewing for humans is invaluable. If you are familiar with basic pattern shapes for such items as trousers, sleeves, and jackets, you can cut your own clothing shapes and sew them directly to your doll. If you like patterns or the idea of removable clothing, start with commercial doll clothing patterns. These can easily be adjusted to fit your doll form. Creating the costume and finishing the doll is where one truly has scope for creativity.

When costuming dolls, the most frequently asked questions are: How do I make hair? How do I make shoes? and How do I make bases?

Traveling Dollmaker by Althea Church; 21", cloth, painted features. Photo by Althea Church.

TOP: *Birdwatching on Stargaze* by Patti Medaris Culea; 18", needlesculpted face, colored with pens and pencils. Photo by Bob Hirsch.

LOWER LEFT: *Ice Princess* by Julie McCullough; 40", needle-sculpted Lycra over velour. Photo by John Nollendorfs.

LOWER RIGHT: *Le Que Sabe (The One Who Knows)* by Melinda Small Paterson; 20", cloth. Photo by Don Smith.

Hair

Let's begin with hair. Just about anything can be used for hair. Hair is usually thought of either as the individual fibers or as the shape of the hairstyle, which gives us two fields of materials and approaches. In most cases, these materials are either glued on (with tacky craft glue) or sewn on. There really are no set methods. The late Robert McKinley, one of the best doll artists in history, if not the best, once described his wigging method to me as follows, "Honey, you just grab a bunch of hair stuff, slap some glue on the head, stick it down, then swoosh it around until it looks right."

Shown here are a few traditional ways of sewing yarn or thread hairstyles. See what effects you could achieve by using some of the "non-traditional" hair materials with them.

RIGHT: Julie McCullough's figure *Sewphie the Stitcher* shows how a fairly basic head and face can become a whimsical personality with the right choice of hair style; 30", cloth. Photo by John Nollendorfs.

LOWER RIGHT: Barbara Evans used her old name tapes and ribbons to create a hair-do for a whimsical doll; 19", cloth. Photo by Barbara Evans.

LOWER LEFT: Many wonderful fibers can be put to good use in creating effect with easily stitched on hair as shown in *Siren* by Deborah Spanton; 16", cloth. Photo by Sherrie Cummins.

Doll Hair Materials

raffia broom straw
(both fuzzy and stalk ends)

flax (natural linen fiber)

bristles (from all sorts of brushes)

yarn
(especially designer fiber mixes)

unraveled yarn
(makes nice curly hair)

string (from unraveled twine to
bakery package string)

ribbon

bunches of mixed ribbons

curled silk ribbon
(use scissors to curl)

mohair

washed and dyed roving
(spun, but unplied)

thread

silk floss

metallic thread

knitting machine cone thread

human hair and synthetic wigs
(cut parts of woven wig caps
to fit doll, then take apart strips
and re-sew to fit doll)

fibers pulled from fabrics

plastic bags
(cut into strips sewn on
in wads)

Easter basket "grass"

tassels

pom-poms

chenille stems

beads

buttons

silk flower petals and leaves

laces
(varying lengths and patterns)

shoe laces

leather strips

pipe cleaners

fabric

braided strips

knotted strips

yo-yos (fabric)

felt
(rolled into curls, or cut
into fringe)

stuffed fabric shapes

fringe

dryer lint

fur, long and short
(natural on skins or
synthetic fabric)

sheepskin

polyester batting

cotton balls

scouring pads (copper)

chains

wood shavings

feathers

beads on wire

…and floor sweepings from
under your sewing machine!

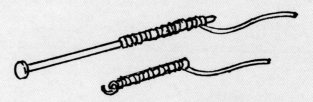

To make yarn curls, wind yarn on a metal knitting needle. Wet the yarn, then dry in a home oven at a low temperature setting.

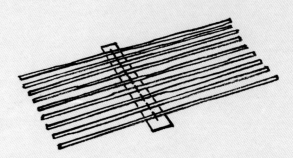

Human hair from purchased wigs can be washed, conditioned, and set using setting preparations and curlers, and then sewn on a fabric strip.

Wefted strips may be sewn or glued directly to a cloth head.

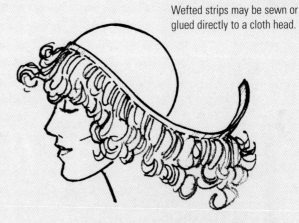

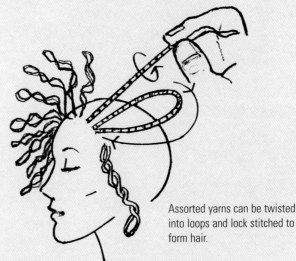

Assorted yarns can be twisted into loops and lock stitched to form hair.

Shoes

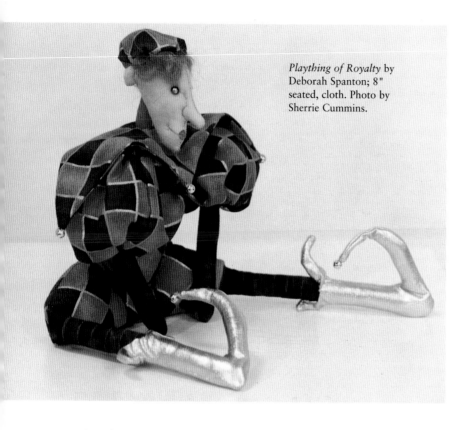

Plaything of Royalty by Deborah Spanton; 8" seated, cloth. Photo by Sherrie Cummins.

Peachy to the Moon by Ellen Turner; 20", cloth. Photo by Don Smith.

Sassy by Genii Townsend; 19", felt over sculpted mask face. Photo by Donald Champion.

Debut: Lady on Staircase by Jane Darin; 21", cloth. When Jane created this scene, the concept of a lady descending a staircase, and the idea of "debut," meant that the step being taken and the shoe taking it had to be as detailed as any of the other parts. Photo by Joe Darin.

The shoes can be made an integral part of the body. Shown here are a few traditional ways of creating shoes. Try different methods using different materials.

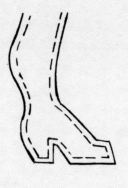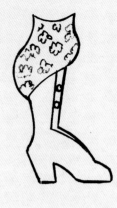

Decide a shoe outline and cut out the shoe shape from a different fabric, adding a ¼" seam allowance.

Seam the fabric to the leg piece.

You can paint shoes right onto the leg fabric. The stockings may be painted as well.

Add embellishments to devise a shoe.

A two-piece foot is given width by adding a cardboard inner sole, essentially making a two-sided stuffed foot into a three-sided foot…with a flat bottom.

Figures with flat soles or very low heels, if firmly stuffed, will stand without external support.

Lay the leg pattern on the cardboard. Draw a line from the heel center to the center of the toe. Cut one pair for the inner soles and another for the outer soles.

Sew and stuff the leg, leaving the open sole at the foot. Insert the cardboard inner form and trim as necessary to fit the shape. Run gathering stitches around the opening. Pull the raw edges over the cardboard inner sole.

DETAIL

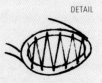

Sew in a criss-cross fashion to secure the edges across the sole. Glue the outer sole over the foot bottom.

Bases

As dollmakers and collectors become more aware of the figure as a piece of art, they want a totally finished look and a secure base for permanent display. Remember, there is no rule that says all dolls are shown standing straight up on a purchased metal stand. Some might, but the joy of the doll is that it can be shown doing just about anything and in any way. As an art piece, the method of display is what can make or break an effective piece.

The most common way of showing a doll is on a wood base, which has either been stained, painted, or covered with fabric. Many ideas for bases and supports can be found in scrap and junk piles...keep your eyes and mind open. I have effectively used lazy Susan bases, wire candelabra, wooden salad bowls and any number of odd items found in the thrift stores. Sometimes the things you find for display will actually give you the idea for the figure to go in or on.

Ideas: A play doll can go in a trunk and have furniture and accessories, a play doll can have a dollhouse, a play doll can have a cloth traveling case or a decorative box. A play doll can have a nice wood or fabric covered base or it could have its own coordinating quilt. Any doll wearing a coated or skirted costume can have a little pocket sewn under its clothing where one could put its story or other information. Doll figures can be built into boxes, picture frames, or hanging structures. A doll can loll on your piano, can hide behind the front door, or can sit in a chair at the dining table. Dust, of course; you have to do it regularly, but, if done carefully, a doll can be vacuumed. Many rag dolls actually look better after a run through the washing machine. However, always take care not to leave a doll exposed to direct sunlight as this can cause the fabrics to fade. Who says a doll just has to be planted...let it fly, let it peek out of a frame. Dolls don't have to be encased in museum displays either, just let them live with you.

Night Fright by Barbara Buysse; 12", painted cloth. Photo by Don Smith.

UNICEF Children by Ellen Rixford; life-sized, needle-sculpture over wire armature. Photo by Ellen Rixford.

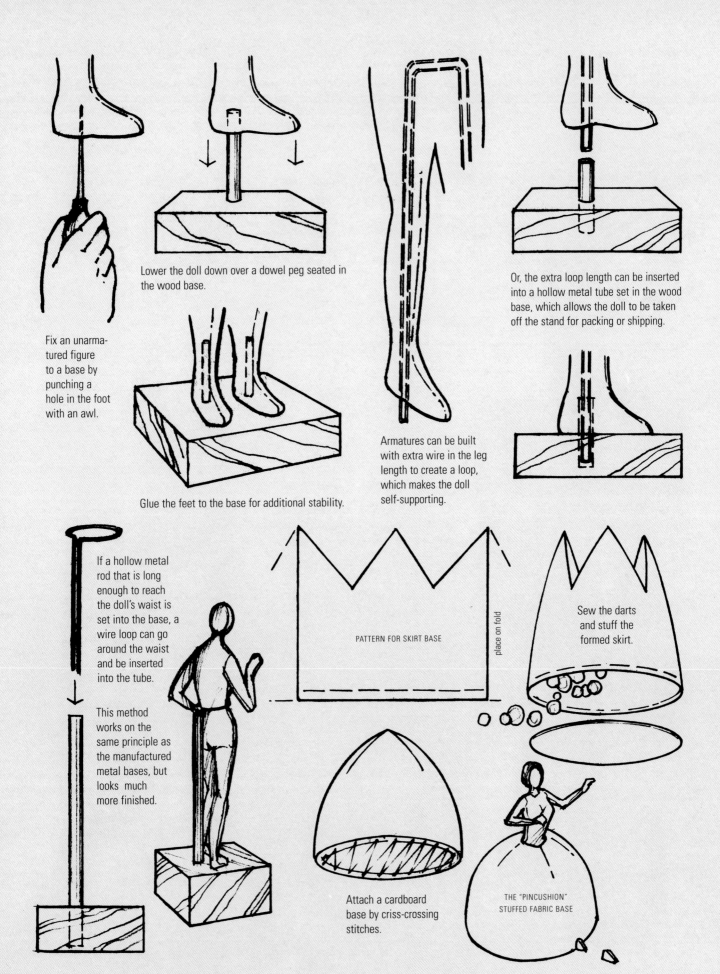

Lower the doll down over a dowel peg seated in the wood base.

Fix an unarmatured figure to a base by punching a hole in the foot with an awl.

Glue the feet to the base for additional stability.

Armatures can be built with extra wire in the leg length to create a loop, which makes the doll self-supporting.

Or, the extra loop length can be inserted into a hollow metal tube set in the wood base, which allows the doll to be taken off the stand for packing or shipping.

If a hollow metal rod that is long enough to reach the doll's waist is set into the base, a wire loop can go around the waist and be inserted into the tube.

This method works on the same principle as the manufactured metal bases, but looks much more finished.

PATTERN FOR SKIRT BASE

place on fold

Sew the darts and stuff the formed skirt.

Attach a cardboard base by criss-crossing stitches.

THE "PINCUSHION" STUFFED FABRIC BASE

Embellishments

BEADS, FEATHERS, BUTTONS, LACE, TRIMS, RIBBONS, FLOWERS, CHAINS, TASSELS, CORDS, SPOOLS, CHARMS, RIBBON FLOWERS, RIBBON EMBROIDERY, CROCHET, KNIT, WEAVING, PAINTING, PRINTING, PHOTOS, DYING STICKS, STONES, DRIED MATERIALS, PINE CONES, THISTLES, GRASSES, BONES, BOTTLE CAPS, SMASHED CANS, SPONGES, LUFFA, COPPER POT SCRUBBERS, POPSICLE STICKS...

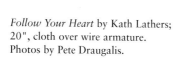

Follow Your Heart by Kath Lathers; 20", cloth over wire armature. Photos by Pete Draugalis.

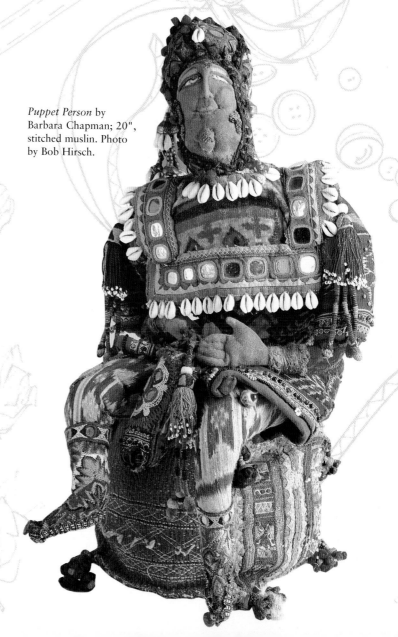

Puppet Person by Barbara Chapman; 20", stitched muslin. Photo by Bob Hirsch.

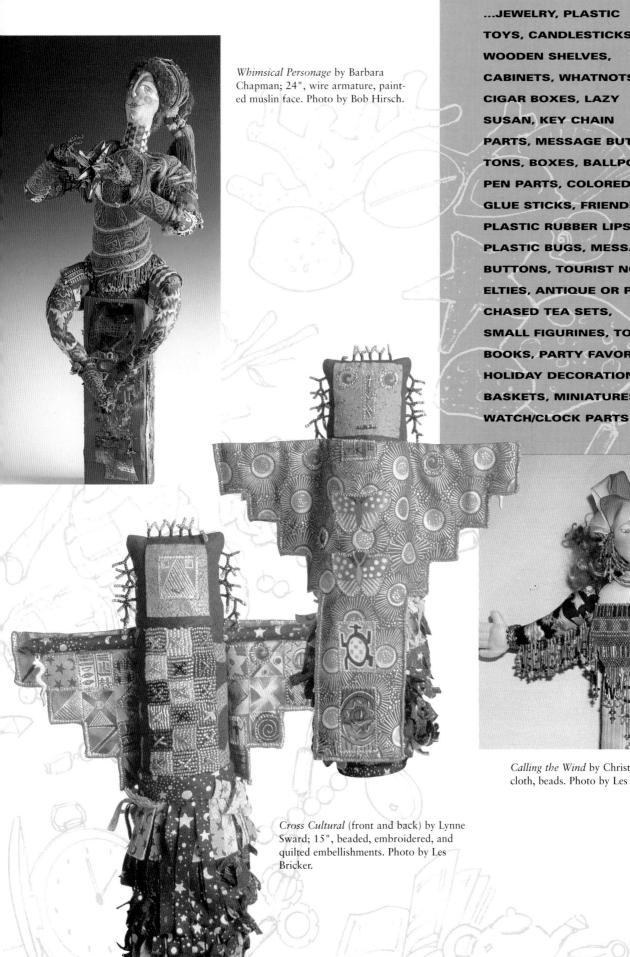

Whimsical Personage by Barbara Chapman; 24", wire armature, painted muslin face. Photo by Bob Hirsch.

...JEWELRY, PLASTIC TOYS, CANDLESTICKS, WOODEN SHELVES, CABINETS, WHATNOTS, CIGAR BOXES, LAZY SUSAN, KEY CHAIN PARTS, MESSAGE BUTTONS, BOXES, BALLPOINT PEN PARTS, COLORED GLUE STICKS, FRIENDLY PLASTIC RUBBER LIPS, PLASTIC BUGS, MESSAGE BUTTONS, TOURIST NOVELTIES, ANTIQUE OR PURCHASED TEA SETS, SMALL FIGURINES, TOYS, BOOKS, PARTY FAVORS, HOLIDAY DECORATIONS, BASKETS, MINIATURES, WATCH/CLOCK PARTS

Calling the Wind by Christine Shively; 16", cloth, beads. Photo by Les Bricker.

Cross Cultural (front and back) by Lynne Sward; 15", beaded, embroidered, and quilted embellishments. Photo by Les Bricker.

Teaching Yourself the ABC's of Dollmaking

Nubian Dancers by Marcella Welch; 36", cloth. Photo by Jerry Anthony.

The best way to learn is to do. Learning will be quicker and be more enjoyable if you allow yourself to have ideas, to play with them, and to experiment with the techniques. In this way you teach yourself to discover and develop your own ideas, and you use the methods which come naturally to you.

Once upon a time a lady who was commissioning me to do a portrait refused to send me a picture of the person. She gave a verbal description and said that she did not want to "mess up my mind with the reality" of a photo. The following exercises have no sketches and no step-by-step drawings because I would rather you made your own dollmaking realities.

Remember, it takes time and failure to master any technique. You are not performing to get a grade or to achieve perfection. If you don't like something the first time, do it again, and again, until you do.

A. DESIGN

Coordinating colors, textures, and finishes. Find an art print or picture that suggests a good doll subject. This should be an illustration where the artist has used paint, pencil, or chalk. Study the face and hands and decide what art medium was used—oils, watercolor, colored pencils, opaque or acrylic color. Look at the facial features and decide what method would be best to reproduce them: embroidery, ink or pencil, appliqué? Study the face and hands and decide what fabric you know of that would either (a) have the same look and feel as the picture or (b) could be painted to have the same look. Study the hair and decide what type of fiber you would use to make a doll's hairstyle to achieve the same look. Look at the clothing and note what fabrics and trims you would use.

Design exercise: Get a pencil and paper, and then pick three dolls shown in the book and try to figure out how the artist created them. Write yourself a set of instructions for making the dolls you selected, including a list of materials and a pattern.

B. ELEMENTAL FORMS

Take a walk around your yard or neighborhood. Collect dried leaves, grasses, twigs, cones, feathers, and pieces of bark. Lay them out and push them around until the bits suggest body parts. Start with a forked stick that suggests a body and legs. Weave or braid leaves and grasses to make costumes. Use feathers to make hair. Use the grasses to twist and secure interesting stones. If you do not have immediate access to the outdoors, have a look at your trash and experiment with plastic bags and containers.

C. COOKIE CUTTER

The adult dollmaker with no prior experience of pattern making will find it helpful to think of the basic flat doll form as one member of a chain of paper dolls. To design your own form, fold a piece of paper in half, sketch a simple half shape, and cut out. Open the piece of paper for a full pattern. If you don't like the shape, fold the paper and trim to suit your eye....or make a few more.

Drawn or painted embellishments are more easily done before sewing and stuffing. When finished with drawing and painting, cut out the pieces and sew them together. Turn and stuff through opening, hand sew to close. What can you do with this form? Christmas tree ornament, pot holder, a wearable pin, string to make a lei, appliqué on clothing...or whatever else can you think of. Make a few to have on hand for experimenting with new fabric colorings, paints, and pens, or for experimenting with faces and surface design ideas.

D. STUFFED DRAWING

On a large piece of newspaper, use a felt pen to draw the simple outline of a figure in motion. Try an acrobat or a dancer. Check the curves in your drawing to make sure they are not too acute. Think about how small a curve can be sewn and turned without a large amount of pucker. Trace your pattern on a doubled piece of scrap fabric, such as old sheeting. Sew, turn, and stuff this test piece to check your curves. Redraw your paper pattern if necessary to make it more pleasing and easy to sew and turn. When you are satisfied that your pattern will work to portray the shape you desire, trace it on your good fabric and complete.

Try again with another figure. This time, piece your fabric, both the back and front sides of the doll, as you would a quilt block. You might start by piecing in a different color for the skirt, or by using a flesh-colored fabric for the head, arms, and legs.

E. SIMPLE JOINTS

Referring to the drawings in this book and using your own imagination, draw a pattern for a simple rag form. Experiment with decreasing or increasing amounts of stuffing at the top of the leg and the arm. Note how the hang of the limbs is changed from very floppy to fairly stiff by the amount of stuffing used. By the way, if these exercise figures are made small (ten inches tall or less), you can embellish them and use them for wearables.

F. FACE PAINTING

Collect at least 6" square scraps of the following: plain weave cotton, linen-like fabric, silk, velvet and/or lightweight velour. Practice sketching and painting faces with watercolor, acrylics, and colored inks. Notice what happens to each fabric. Note which fabrics tend to bleed color. Keep a scrap bag going and every once in awhile treat yourself to an hour of experimenting with faces and mediums. Some of these practice pieces will turn into very interesting dolls!

G. NEEDLESCULPTING COTTON

Cut, sew, and stuff six or more heads of the center seam nose type (page 31) using plain woven cotton and then practice your needlesculpture stitches (page 46). Vary your practice by making heads of plain weave cotton, felt, and knit. Notice how the same stitch patterns will result in different sculpted effects on different fabric types.

H. NEEDLESCULPTING NYLON STOCKING FABRIC

Cut two-way stretch panty hose into sections about 8" long. Stuff each section and gather each end to close. Practice your needlesculpture stitches (page 42). If necessary, cut a small hole in the back or open an end to add more stuffing. After you have done several with this method, see what happens if you sew a flat head of cotton fabric and then attach the stocking fabric face to the front of it. Or, try constructing a fully round head, pulling the stocking fabric over it and stuffing as necessary. Secure the needlesculpting stitches by sewing into a solid stuffed head.

I. SIMPLE FACE CONTOURS WITH CLAY

Construct at least six heads using the contoured method (page 33). Use doubled thread to create the eye-line contour. Use air-drying clay to build a nose and the chin area (page 49). When the clay material is dry, cover the face area with a light coat of craft glue and cover the face with a loose weave or stretchy fabric.

J. MASK FACES

Use oven-cured polymer clays or air-drying paperclays to sculpt a simple face mask form. Make several. Experiment with a variety of covering materials, such as cotton gauze, muslin, stockinette knits, swimsuit knits, or even leather.

Stand Up by Beverly Dodge Radefeld; 18", cloth. Photo by Beverly Dodge Radefeld.

Experiment with the effects of (a) painting the face, (b) insetting beads or purchased glass or plastic eyes, or (c) creating a separate eyelid. Ask yourself how you would create an open mouth. Always leave an overlap of at least ½" of covering fabric at the edge so that the mask can be attached to a stuffed head form by stitching.

K. SHAPING THE TORSO

Look at the various methods of shaping a bust. Then think of at least two more variations for each method (different shapes, different fabrics, different methods of attachment). Try them!

L. MAKING REALISTIC HANDS

Enlarge the hand pattern with fingers (page 77). Cut several patterns and practice sewing, cutting, turning, and stuffing them. See how small you can make a hand.

M. PRACTICING FOOT AND SHOE CONSTRUCTION

Construct a pair of legs and feet for as many foot designs as you can find in this book.

N. THE TIED JOINT

Stuff each limb to the joint. Hold the stuffing back firmly and tie the limb so the knot rests firmly against stuffed area. Try weighting the feet and hands, but do not stuff between joints.

O. THE BEAD JOINT

Study the stitched bead joint diagrams (page 103) and observe the forms of the undressed dolls made by Shelley Thornton (page 102) and Maggie Iacono (page 98). Then invent your own versions.

P. THE GUSSETED BUTTON JOINT

The illustrations of the gusseted joint (page 107) show the gusset in the upper limb. Try designing a pattern to make the gusset or attachment tab for the lower limb.

Q. DESIGNING BUTTON JOINTS

Can you re-design this joint (page 107) to be easier to make? How many joint variations can you make? How small can you make them? How would you joint a head?

R. WIRE ARMATURE

Construct several wire armatures (page 110) about 8" tall to get the feel of what is required to work with wire. Bend figures into different poses. Do the poses suggest particular actions or characters? Tear printed cotton fabric into half strips and practice wrapping wire bodies. As you wrap, take care to "sculpt" by wrapping thinly at joint areas and by wrapping several times at body parts where thickness is required. Add beads, buttons, or other embellishment materials and create a series of wearables.

Try covering a wire armature by wrapping it with cotton string or yarn. Wrap the string so that the strands flatten as you wrap. When the wire has been sculpted with the wrapped string to a full body shape, cut the felt pieces and cover the body by hand stitching felt around the limbs.

S. WIRE ARMATURED BODIES

Design or pick a basic cloth figure pattern. Cut, sew, and turn pieces. Lay unstuffed pieces out, overlapping parts about ½" (twice the amount of seam allowance). Construct a wire armature to fit inside the body pieces. Check the sizing of the armature by laying it over the unstuffed pieces. Then insert the armature into the body as if putting on a shirt. Stuff. Pull the arms and legs over the wire, and stuff and sew to the body at the shoulder and hip. When the body is stuffed around the wire, the stuffing will expand or widen the body. This means that the armature will need to be a little shorter than the pattern. Each type of fabric and your method of stuffing will produce different results. Be ready to adjust or to repeat until your armature fits the body.

T. FIXED BASE FIGURES
Select three or more pieces of woven printed cotton that you have had for a long time, but perhaps never liked or found a good use for. Study the fabrics and let the patterns or colors tell you what sort of dolls they would like to be. With a wood block and a coat hanger, construct a fixed figure (page 117). Design a simple body form to go over the armature and pick a style for the head and hands that matches your figure concept. Complete the figure using whatever finishes and embellishments seem needed.

U. THE CONTOURED HEAD
Construct two or three contoured heads (page 33). Then make two or three more. See what happens (a) if you appliqué a nose (b) if you needlesculpt the corners of the mouth, or (c) if you paint the head with a very thick layer of paint.

V. BODY CONTOURS
Nancy Laverick's contoured figures were suggested to her by odd shaped scraps on her sewing room floor. Cut or find a few odd-shaped pieces of fabric—at least two of them should be identical. Measure around the outside edges and cut a ribbon of fabric about 2" wide and as long as your measurement, plus 1" for the seam allowance. Sew one side of ribbon to one piece (right sides together), and sew the other side of the ribbon to the other piece. Is this confusing? Try looking at the photos to figure it out (page 66).

W. COVERING A BODY
Contruct a jointed doll. Experiment with covering or "making an outer skin" for it. Use stretchy fabrics and needlesculpt to emphasize muscle definition.

X. BODY DARTS
Design an arm with a simple form in a straight position. Cut two pieces and sew a dart at the inside elbow bend of each piece. Put the pieces right sides together, and then sew, turn, and stuff. The dart will create a bent arm. Vary the width of the dart to achieve maximum bend. Compare the darted elbow (and knee) to a pattern where the bend is designed into the form of the basic pattern.

Y. BODY GUSSETS
A two-piece doll pattern is often "too skinny" in the calf or the leg and thigh. What happens if you construct a long triangular gusset making a third leg back piece?

Z. FINISHING THINGS
Take all your practice pieces and lay them out on a table. Push them around to see how many complete or nearly complete dolls you have from the parts. Decide how each might be completed. Think about working colors and textures to pull parts together. Think about what is missing and what you might do to fill in the missing part. Let the fabrics, shapes, and faces suggest ideas to you. What you complete will be your own original dolls. Consider which methods you enjoyed doing and which worked best for you. It is most likely that the methods you liked will be the best for you to develop in your own designs.

Ancestors by Anne Mayer Meier; 32" to 34", fabric with modeled clay faces. Photo by Photo Pro.

APPENDIX B
Sources

The best means of finding out what is happening in the doll world and what is available is to subscribe to one or two periodicals. All of them provide valuable information, articles, updates of current events, and most provide patterns and technical tips.

A dollmaker can never have or read enough books. From books we learn what other dollmakers have done and what they are doing, as well as the technical processes associated with our craft. Most of the books available from large, commercial publishers are carried by the book distributors listed below. Write and ask for their catalog of titles.

Hobby House Press
1 Corporate Drive
Grantsville, MD 21536

Scott Publications
30595 Eight Mile Road
Livonia, MI 48152

Unfortunately, many valuable dollmaking books have limited print life and many more are privately printed and difficult to locate. Many interesting patterns are self-published by artists and only a small percentage can be regularly stocked by fabric and craft shops. On the artist list below, we have keyed(*/#) those who teach and/or sell patterns and books. If you write an artist for information, be sure to include a stamped, addressed envelope for the reply. For a few stamps and envelopes, you will find a whole new world of dollmaking opportunities.

ARTISTS

* = Patterns/books sold
# = Available to teach classes

Angelique, Lawan
2458 West Bayshore Road #7
Palo Alto, CA 94303

Anzai, Akiko
1609 Treehouse Lane
Roanoke, TX 76262

Asami, Keiko
150 Shimokagemori, Chichibu
Saitama, 369-18 Japan

Austin, Sara
3301 Via La Selva
Palos Verdes Estates, CA 90274

*# bailey, elinor peace
1779 East Avenue
Hayward, CA 94541

Ballentine, Betty
1863 Pioneer Parkway East #121
Springfield, OR 97477

Bates, Jeanie
21978 S.W. Creek Drive
Tualatin, OR 97062

*# Belt, Sandy
6612 US 41 South
Marquette, MI 49855

Belzer, Kathryn
RR2 Schubenacadie, Nova Scotia
Canada, BON 2HO

Black, Virginia
12650 Hortense Street
Studio City, CA 91604

Blount, Akira
P.O. Box 87
Bybee, TN 37713

*# Boots, Bonnie
330 28th Street North
St. Petersburg, FL 33713

Bouse, Kareena
25484 Lake Wohlford Road
Box 168
Escondido, CA 92027

Buysse, Barbara
9630 Almena
Kalamazoo, MI 49009

Cannon, Margery
985 Vista View Drive
Salt Lake City, UT 84108

Carlin, Caty
P.O. Box 214
Penland, NC 28765

*# Casey, Jacqueline
Route 2, Box 405
Murphy, NC 28906

*# Cely, Antonette
3592 Cherokee Road
Atlanta, GA 30340

Chapman, Barbara
353 Glenmont Drive
Solana Beach, CA 92075

Church, Althea
14 Dudley St. #4
Arlington, MA 02174

Cokely, Molly
P.O. Box 1564
Lafayette, CA 94549

Coleman-Cobb, Patricia
P.O. Box 11287
Elkins Park, PA 19027

Craver, Becky
20618 Lehmans Mill Road
Hagerstown, MD 21742

Culea, Patti Medaris
9019 Stargaze Avenue
San Diego, CA 92129

Darin, Jane
4757 Edison Street
San Diego, CA 92117

Davies, Jane
Amber The Street
Walberton, Arundel, Sussex
England BNI8 0PH

Denn, Marlene
P.O. Box 317
New Lathrop, MI 48460

Dunn, Andra
12 Geary Avenue
Fairfax, CA 94930

Evans, Barbara
132 Poli Street
Ventura, CA 93001

Ewing, Linda
13101 Chrisco
Saugus, CA 91350

Feingold, Sandra
1752 Gascony Road
Encinitas, CA 92024

Fiebing, Kate
841 S. Ridgeview Trail
Suttons Bay, MI 49682

Florio, Marla
24373 Fairway Hills Drive
Novi, MI 48374

Flynn, Peggy
1920 N. Kilpatrick
Portland, OR 97217

Fulton, Catherine
1275-99 North Gilbert Street
Fullerton, CA 92633

Gehl, Brenda
N89 W15283 Cleveland Ave #3
Menomonee Falls, WI 53051

*# Gourley, Miriam
1033 N. 560 E.
Orem, UT 84057

Hale, Susan
8473 Kaehlers Mill Road
Cedarburg, WI 53012

Hastings, Pamela
161 Wilhelm Road
Saugerties, NY 12477

Hennen, Margi
363 St. James Street
London, Ontario
Canada N6A1X8

*# Hoover, Bonnie
26889 Lakewood Way
Hayward, CA 94544

Iacono, Maggie
2 Raymond Circle
Dowingtown, PA 19335

Irick, Terry
945 Aruba Lane
Foster City, CA 94404

Katin, Hedy
P.O. Box 309
Yankeetown, FL 34498

Kinsey, Dawn
Box 938
Three Hills, Alberta
Canada, TOM 2A0

Knoop, Fayette
P.O. Box 237
North Freedom, WI 53951

*# Lampi, Sally
2261 Beckham Way
Hayward, CA 94541

* Landis, Ruth
1185 Arroyo Grande Drive
Sacramento, CA 95816

Lathers, Kath
37220 Eight Mile Road
Farmington, MI 48335

*# Laverick, Nancy
6517-D Four Winds Drive
Charlotte, NC 28212

*# Lichtenfels, Lisa
P.O. Box 90537
Springfield, MA 01139

Liesfeld, Junko
12346 Casco Mill Lane
Montpelier, VA 23192

Lima, Gretchen
1419 S. 20th Street
Sheboygan, WI 53081

Malerich, Norma
2200 S. Ocean Blvd #902
Delray Beach, FL 33483

*# Matsubara, Toyoko
3-36 Asahigaoka-Cho, Suita
Osaka, Japan 564

* Matthews, Kezi
P.O. Box 17631
Portland, OR 97217

Mayer, Maggie
718 S.W. Bay Pointe Circle
Palm City, FL 34990

*# McCullough, Julie
719 P Street
Lincoln, NE 68508

Meier, Anne Mayer
169 Sandalwood Way
Longwood, FL 32750

Mendenhall, Louise
4714 Mullen Road
New Bern, NC 28560

Ogawa, Sizuyo
Komatsushi-Jonanmachi 106
Ishikawa Ken, Japan

*# Oroyan, Susanna
3270 Whitbeck Boulevard
Eugene, OR 97405

*# Paterson, Melinda Small
10465 N.W. Lee Court
Portland, OR 97229

Patterson, Joyce
P.O. Box 1599
Brazoria, TX 77422

Petefish, Frances
8630 Anrol Avenue
San Diego, CA 92123

Pitkin, Doree
2019 26th Avenue
Greeley, CO 80631

* Porcella, Yvonne
3619 Shoemake Avenue
Modesto, CA 95358

Port, Beverly
P.O. Box 711
Retsil, WA 98378

Pringle, Helen
2188 Annetta C. P. Road
Aledo, TX 76008

Radefeld, Beverly Dodge
10650 NW 13th
Topeka, KS 66615

Riley, Lesley
7814 Hampden Lane
Bethesda, MD 20814

*# Rixford, Ellen
308 West 97th Street
New York, NY 10025

*# Robertson, Virginia
Box 490
Overbrook, KS 66524

Sargeant, Dinah
23725 Via Lupona
Valencia, CA 91355

Sasaki, Akiko
3-5-14 Kamiichi, Kashiwara-Shi
Osaka, Japan 582

*# Sawyer, Joyce
P.O. Box 803
Nashville, IN 47448

Schklar, Lois
140 A Euclid Avenue
Toronto, Ontario
Canada M6J 2J9

*# Shattil, Deb
9200 Skyline Boulevard
Oakland, CA 94611

Shively, Christine
112 Hilltop Road
Ozawkie, KS 66070

Spanton, Deborah
10655 South West Collina
Portland, OR 97219

Spence, Elaine Anne
1513 Holly Street
West Linn, OR 97068

* Spencer, Barbara
Route 5, Box 165A
Oakview Addition
El Dorado Springs, MO 64744

Stewart, Bonnie
4875 Cole Street #40
San Diego, CA 92117

Stillwell, Tracy Page
85 Horseneck Road
Warwick, RI 02886

Stygles, Carol
3375 Hoyer Road
Jackson, MI 49201

Swanson, Rebecca
802 Lincoln Way
Auburn, CA 95603

Sward, Lynne
625 Bishop
Virginia Beach, VA 23455

*# Takahashi, Tomiko
5-8-704 Mihama Urayasusi
Tibaken, Japan

*# Thomas, Mary
122 Brookside Place
Marinia, CA 93933

Thompson, Carla
102 Canterbury Circle
Madison, AL 35758

Thornton, Shelley
1600 S. 22nd Street
Lincoln, NE 68502

Tidwell-Foutz, Katheryn
565 Los Osos Valley Road
Los Osos, CA 93402

Townsend, Genii
3710 W. Spinnaker Lane
Tucson, AZ 85742

Wagner, Jane
3345 Munsel Lake Road # 24
Florence, Or 97439

Waugh, Carol-Lynn Rössel
5 Morrill Street
Winthrop, ME 04364

Welch, Marcella
5475 Route 193
Andover, OH 44003

Westling, Charlene
3228 N.W. Alice Drive
Topeka, KS 66618

*# Willis, Barbara
415 Palo Alto
Mountain View, CA 94041

*# Winer, Gloria
P.O. Box 662
Point Pleasant, NJ 08742

Wood, Zhenne
4701 San Leandro #35
Oakland, CA 97601

Woodman, Ann
2030 Crest Mar Circle
El Dorado Hills, CA 95762

Wooten, Karen
12606 Stoutwood St.
Poway, CA 92064

Yamamoto, Mitsuko
6-21-5-205 Tsukagosh
Warabi-city, Saitama-ken
Japan 355

SUPPLIES

Cotton Patch Mail Order
3405 Hall Lane, Dept. CTB
Lafayette, CA 94549
e-mail: cottonpa@aol.com
(800) 835-4418
(510) 383-7882
Assorted tools, fabric, wool
roving, and stuffing

BIBLIOGRAPHY

Litchenfels, Lisa, *The Basic Head: Soft Sculpture Techniques* (self-published, 1991).

Shakespeare, William, *A Midsummer Night's Dream* (New York, Bantam, 1988).

ABOUT
the Author

Susanna Oroyan taught herself the art of dollmaking. Since 1972, she has made over 500 dolls, and her dollmaking has become a full-time career and a business. For the past decade, Susanna has been a motivating force in regional and national dollmakers' organizations. She has exhibited her dolls internationally and has written several books, including *Fantastic Figures* by C&T Publishing, and well over two hundred articles for doll magazines. She has also taught dollmaking classes at many major seminars as well as for individual dollmaking groups. Susanna's cloth-doll patterns are available from:

Fabricat Designs
3270 Whitbeck Boulevard
Eugene, OR 97405

Other Fine Books From C&T Publishing:

An Amish Adventure: 2nd Edition, Roberta Horton
Appliqué 12 Easy Ways! Elly Sienkiewicz
Art & Inspirations: Judith Baker Montano, Judith Baker Montano
Art & Inspirations: Ruth B. McDowell, Ruth B. McDowell
The Art of Silk Ribbon Embroidery, Judith Baker Montano
The Artful Ribbon: Beauties in Bloom, Candace Kling
Baltimore Beauties and Beyond (2 Volumes), Elly Sienkiewicz
Basic Seminole Patchwork, Cheryl Greider Bradkin
Beyond the Horizon: Small Landscape Appliqué, Valerie Hearder
Buttonhole Stitch Appliqué, Jean Wells
Colors Changing Hue, Yvonne Porcella
Crazy Quilt Handbook, Judith Baker Montano
Crazy Quilt Odyssey, Judith Baker Montano
Crazy with Cotton: Piecing Together Memories & Themes, Diana Leone
Dimensional Appliqué: Baskets, Blooms & Baltimore Borders, Elly Sienkiewicz
Elegant Stitches: An Illustrated Stitch Guide & Source Book of Inspiration, Judith Baker Montano
Enduring Grace: Quilts from the Shelburne Museum Collection, Celia Y. Oliver
Everything Flowers: Quilts from the Garden, Jean and Valori Wells
The Fabric Makes the Quilt, Roberta Horton
Faces & Places: Images in Appliqué, Charlotte Warr Andersen
Fantastic Figures: Ideas & Techniques Using the New Clays, Susanna Oroyan
Fractured Landscape Quilts, Katie Pasquini Masopust
From Fiber to Fabric: The Essential Guide to Quiltmaking Textiles, Harriet Hargrave
Heirloom Machine Quilting, Harriet Hargrave
Imagery on Fabric: 2nd Edition, Jean Ray Laury
Impressionist Palette, Gai Perry
Kaleidoscopes & Quilts, Paula Nadelstern
Mariner's Compass Quilts: New Directions, Judy Mathieson
Mastering Machine Appliqué, Harriet Hargrave
Nancy Crow: Improvisational Quilts, Nancy Crow
On the Surface, Wendy Hill
The New Sampler Quilt, Diana Leone
Papercuts and Plenty: Vol. III of Baltimore Beauties and Beyond, Elly Sienkiewicz
Patchwork Persuasion: Fascinating Quilts from Traditional Designs, Joen Wolfrom
Pattern Play: Creating Your Own Quilts, Doreen Speckmann
Patchwork Quilts Made Easy, Jean Wells (co-published with Rodale Press, Inc.)
Pieced Clothing Variations, Yvonne Porcella
Pieces of an American Quilt, Patty McCormick
Plaids and Stripes, Roberta Horton
QuiltArt: Visions '96, Quilt San Diego
Quilts for Fabric Lovers, Alex Anderson
Quilts from the Civil War, Barbara Brackman
Quilts, Quilts, and More Quilts! Diana McClun and Laura Nownes
Say It with Quilts, Diana McClun and Laura Nownes
Schoolhouse Appliqué: Reverse Techniques and More, Charlotte Patera
Simply Stars: Quilts that Sparkle, Alex Anderson
Six Color World, Yvonne Porcella
Small Scale Quiltmaking: Precision, Proportion, and Detail, Sally Collins
Soft-Edge Piecing, Jinny Beyer
Start Quilting with Alex Anderson: Six Projects for First-Time Quilters, Alex Anderson
Stripes in Quilts, Mary Mashuta
Symmetry: A Design System for Quiltmakers, Ruth B. McDowell
3 Dimensional Design, Katie Pasquini
Tradition with a Twist: Variations on Your Favorite Quilts, Blanche Young and Dalene Young Stone
Trapunto by Machine, Hari Walner
The Visual Dance: Creating Spectacular Quilts, Joen Wolfrom
Willowood: Further Adventures in Buttonhole Stitch Appliqué, Jean Wells

For more information write for a free catalog from:
C&T Publishing
P.O. Box 1456
Lafayette, CA 94549
(1-800-284-1114)
http://www.ctpub.com

143

INDEX

Ballerina Dolls by Kathy Ross; 1", cloth. Photo by Don Smith.

adult height formula, 110

bases
  inserting dowels, 135
  material, 134
  securing wire to, 117
  wire armature support, 135
  wire waist loop, 135

bust
  appliquéd patch, 71
  contoured, 73
  darted dress form, 71
  undergarment, 73

contoured body, 66, 69

costuming, 18, 64, 116, 128

creativity
  definition, 8, 9, 11
  process, 8, 9

design
  elements of, 8
  Flutterby form, 19
  Flying Phoebe form, 21
  Rag-a-Mama form, 17

doll
  definition, 12, 48
  evolution, 12–14, 16
  visualization, 128

doll challenge
  group, 14
  Midsummer Night's Dream, 8, 9

dollmakers
  Angelique, Lawan, 28, 38, 86
  Anzai, Akiko, 1, 63, 70, 108, cover
  Asami, Keiko, 114
  Austin, Sara, 121
  bailey, elinor peace, 20, 28, 32, 61, 121
  Ballentine, Betty, 24
  Bates, Jeanie, 50, 63, 94
  Belt, Sandy, 26
  Belzer, Kathryn, 46
  Black, Virginia, 24, 34
  Blount, Akira, 58, 87, 104
  Boots, Bonnie, 38, 127
  Bouse Kareena, 95
  Buysse, Barbara, 60, 87, 134
  Cannon, Margery, 40, 80, 95, 108
  Carlin, Caty, 120
  Casey, Jacqueline, 48, 76, 92
  Cely, Antonette, 64, 82, 124
  Chapman, Barbara, 92, 136, 137
  Church, Althea, 18, 128
  Cokely, Molly, 112
  Coleman-Cobb, Patricia, 119
  Craver, Becky, 62, 123
  Culea, Patti Medaris, 119, 129
  Darin, Jane, 43, 104, 132
  Davis, Lenore, 84
  Davies, Jane, 118
  Denn, Marlene, 34
  Dunn, Andra, 58, 62, 122
  Evans, Barbara, 16, 36, 130
  Ewing, Linda, 62
  Feingold, Sandra, 20, 118
  Fiebing, Kate, 30
  Florio, Marla, 125
  Flynn, Peggy, 58, 94, cover

  Fulton, Catherine, 125, 127
  Gehl, Brenda, 9
  Gourley, Miriam, 126
  Hale, Susan, 127
  Hastings, Pamela, 63, 76, 89
  Hennen, Margi, 4, 5, 14, 22, 63
  Hoover, Bonnie, 30, 96
  Iacono, Maggie, 98
  Irick, Terry, 50, 114
  Katin, Hedy, 90
  Kinsey, Dawn, 90, 110, 112
  Knoop, Fayette, 45
  Lampi, Sally, 20, 22, 32, 38, 45, 47
  Landis, Ruth, 80
  Lathers, Kath, 87, 136
  Laverick, Nancy, 66, 120
  Lichtenfels, Lisa, 54, 88, back cover
  Liesfeld, Junko, 40, 68, 124
  Lima, Gretchen, 7, 88
  Malerich, Norma, 26, 61
  Matsubara, Toyoko, 45, 68
  Matthews, Kezi, cover
  Mayer, Maggie, 62, 74, 110, 116, 126
  McCullough, Julie, 63, 91, 92, 96, 129, 130, cover
  Meier, Anne Mayer, 22, 126, 140
  Mendenhall, Louise, 18
  Ogawa, Sizuyo, 18
  Oroyan, Susanna, 3, 9, 10, 11, 26, 32, 34, 36, 58, 63, 72, 78, 96, 100, 104, 112, 116
  Paterson, Melinda Small, 129
  Patterson, Joyce, 30, 93
  Petefish, Frances, 122
  Pitkin, Doree, 40, 72, 95
  Porcella, Yvonne, 94
  Port, Beverly, 61
  Pringle, Helen, 60, 88
  Radefeld, Beverly Dodge, 91, 139
  Riley, Lesley, 34
  Rixford, Ellen, 74, 89, 134
  Robertson, Virginia, 4, 28, 63, 100, 120
  Ross, Kathy, 144
  Sargeant, Dinah, 63
  Sasaki, Akiko, 68, 118
  Sawyer, Joyce, 50
  Schklar, Lois, 7
  Shattil, Deb, 70, 82, 93
  Shively, Christine, 8, 126, 137
  Spanton, Deborah, 62, 130, 132
  Spence, Elaine Anne, 18, 26, 100
  Spencer, Barbara, 63
  Stewart, Bonnie, 123
  Stillwell, Tracy Page, 14, 36, 123
  Stygles, Carol, 90
  Swanson, Rebecca, 24, 48, 62
  Sward, Lynne, 137
  Takahashi, Tomiko, 80, 93, 108, 114
  Thomas, Mary, 47, 62

  Thompson, Carla, 52, 126
  Thornton, Shelley, 89, 102
  Tidwell-Foutz, Katheryn, 30
  Townsend, Genii, 132
  Turner, Ellen, 34, 132
  Wagner, Jane, 18
  Waugh, Carol-Lynn Rössel, 24
  Welch, Marcella, 62, 119, 138
  Westling, Charlene, 61, 74
  Willis, Barbara, 76, 123
  Winer, Gloria, 72, 94
  Wood, Zhenne, 91
  Woodman, Ann, 122
  Wooten, Karen, 82, 124
  Yamamoto, Mitsuko, 125

feet
  all-in-one-shoe, 65, 81, 133
  cardboard sole, 81, 133
  flat sole, 133
  three-piece foot, 81
  two-piece foot, 133

French modeling, 84, 85

gusset
  chin gusset, 33
  limb gusset, 107
  under gusset, 73

hair
  materials, 131
  Robert McKinley wigging method, 130
  wefted strips, 131
  yarn curls, 131

hands
  complex, 69
  defining fingers, 74, 75
  flat fingers, 48
  hiding seams, 48
  moveable fingers, 75
  padded wire, 79
  posing fingers, 79
  simple, 69
  skinny fingers, 74
  wire armature, 77

heads
  appliquéd features, 36, 37
  baseball head, 33
  blended method 54, 55
  flat head, 28
  four-piece head, 31
  fully sculptural head, 34
  long head with gusset, 33
  pressed head, 51
  round head with darts, 33
  two-piece head, 31

joints
  ball and socket, 98, 102, 107
  bead, 100-103
  button, 104-107
  circular movement, 27
  decorative, 96, 97
  hidden, 106
  mortise and tenon, 107
  options, 98, 99
  plastic button set, 105
  quarter turn, 27
  stitched, 27
  strung, 107
  tension, 104
  three-dimensional, 84
  washer and cotter pins, 105

legs
  simple, 69
  contour, 69

masks
  commercial, 52
  preparation, 59

materials
  clay (also paperclay), 15, 22, 48, 49, 50, 52, 53, 58, 59, 114
  corn husk, 15, 17
  creating bases with, 134, 135
  embellishments, 136, 137
  felt, 16, 19
  Fimo, 64
  grasses, 15
  plastic wrap, uses of, 59
  stone, 15
  Styrofoam, 50, 55
  wax, 52
  wire, 17, 108
  wood, 15, 114
  yarn, 16

needlesculpture
  bag ridges, 44
  cheeks, 44
  direct method, 38, 46
  double-threaded needle, 40
  enhanced underlayment, 38, 57
  eyes, 44
  eyelids, blended method, 56
  fabrics for, 40, 52
  facial contours, blended method, 57
  jowls, 44
  mouth, blended method, 56
  mouth, puff, 44
  mouth, straight, 44
  nose, 46
  nose, blended method, 56
  raised features, 38, 42
  simple form, 38
  subsurface stitches, 42, 57
  typical stitches, 42

painting
  watercolor, 60
  acrylic, 60
  tinting, 60
  priming, 60, 61
  sealers, 61

pattern draping, 84, 85

pattern guides
  baseball head, 33
  basic body, 65
  basic foot, 81
  contoured body, 67, 69
  foot with dimensional toe, 81
  fully sculptural head, 35
  outline form, 29
  pincushion skirt, 135
  rag doll, 25
  rolled felt, 19
  round head, 33
  three-piece nose, 37
  two-piece ear, 37
  whole body, sloper, 84, 85

wire
  covering, 114, 115
  fixed, 116, 117
  inserting, 112, 113
  twisting, 109
  types, 108
  wrapping, 109, 111, 114, 115